W9-CCB-594

Blender Cooking

Publisher: R. Arthur Barrett
Edited by Margaret W. Madine
Art Director Dick Collins   Photography by Bill Miller

trp®

TESTED RECIPE PUBLISHERS, INC. CHICAGO

Table of Contents

REVISED ENLARGED EDITION
FOURTH PRINTING

Library of Congress Catalog Card Number 68-28983

Published in U.S.A. by Tested Recipe Publishers, Inc., 6701 Oakton St., Chicago, Ill. 60648. Printed in U.S.A. by American Printers & Lithographers, Inc., Chicago, Ill. 60648.

Introduction

The blenders of today are designed for the modern homemaker. The blender is truly a kitchen appliance that can be of use in practically every food preparation step. In seconds, not minutes, the blender can **STIR, CRUMB, PUREE, WHIP, GRATE, MIX, CHOP, GRIND, BLEND, OR LIQUEFY.** This blender book is adaptable to all blenders old or new.

Recipe Speeds In This Book

The recipes in this book use a speed range from 1 to 13. Speeds are shown in **LARGER** type. **If your blender** does not have 13 speeds you will need a cross-reference. The chart below (after you complete the outer portion for **your** blender speeds) will be your cross-reference.

Completing Speed Chart For Your Blender

1. If your blender speed settings **are on** the chart below:
   Find the section of the chart that has the same number of speeds as your blender. Extend the lines between the various speeds out to the outer blank section of the chart. Write in **your** blender settings in the spaces in the outer section. Chart is now ready to use.

2. If your blender's speeds **are not on** the chart below:
   Divide the outer blank section into the same number of spaces as speeds on your blender. Write in your blender settings in the spaces in the outer section. Chart is now ready to use.

How To Use The Completed Chart

1. Find the **recipe speed** in the portion of the chart titled **"Recipe Speeds In This Book."**

2. Use **your** speed in the outer area opposite **"Recipe Speeds In This Book."** (You may even want to write **your** speed on the recipe itself.)

3. Fill out the removable chart on the back cover page and place it near your blender work area for future reference.

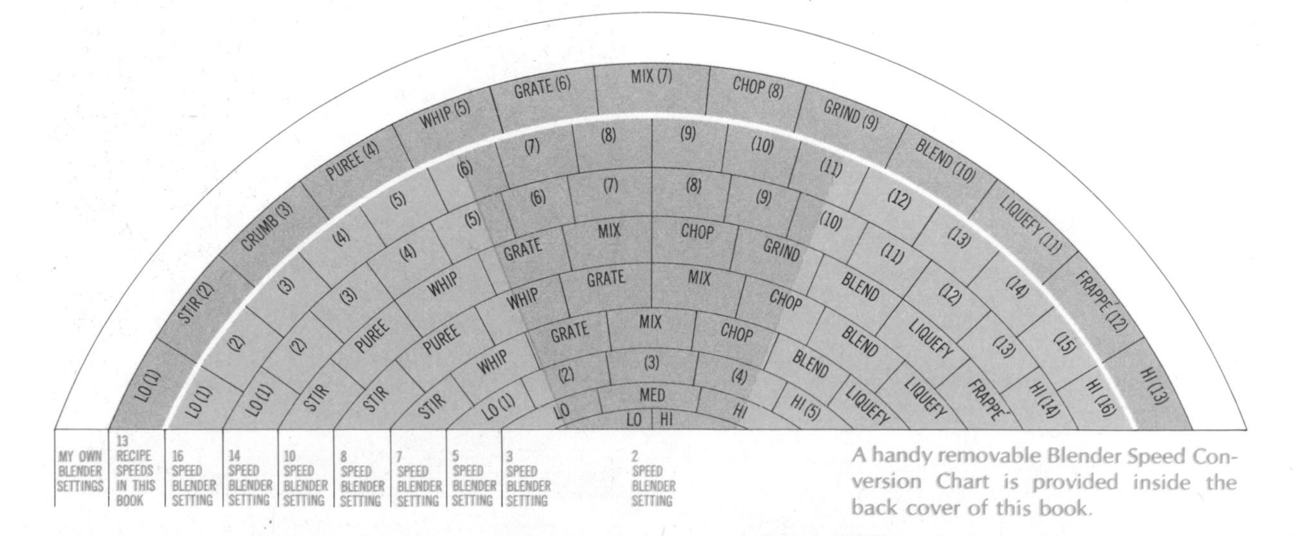

A handy removable Blender Speed Conversion Chart is provided inside the back cover of this book.

Blender Techniques

1. **Read manufacturer's instructions before using.**

2. Set blender on a clean dry surface before starting motor. This will keep foreign particles from being drawn into motor.

3. Set container firmly in place on the base. Cover; rest hand lightly on cover while starting motor (Fig. 1).

4. Always put liquid and semi-liquid ingredients into container first, unless recipe states otherwise.

5. Caution: some blenders require the motor to be running before solid or semi-solid ingredients are added to container. Use small **top opening** in cover when adding ingredients.

6. Slice or dice firm fruits, vegetables, cooked meats, etc., into ¾ to 1-inch cubes or pieces before adding to container. Cut hard and natural cheeses into ½-inch cubes. Cut very cold ice cream or frozen fruits into 1-inch cubes or pieces.

7. Cool very hot foods slightly before adding to container unless recipe states otherwise.

8. Underblend! **The blender chops lightning fast!** For coarsely chopped mixtures, stop motor often and examine for particle size or switch motor "on-and-off" several times until particles of desired size are obtained. Watch closely!

9. If your blender doesn't have a timer, count processing time in seconds! Watch the second hand of the kitchen clock or count 1001, 1002, 1003, 1004, etc.

10. Make foods in small batches. Usually it's easier and it takes only seconds to make each batch.

11. Pour liquid and semi-liquid mixtures out of pitcher-like container. Heavy mixtures are easier to remove through bottom opening on blenders and containers with removable processing assemblies.

12. Clean and dry container and processing assembly immediately after each use and reassemble.

Figure 1

13. **Rubber spatula technique for stiff mixtures:** Stop motor; push ingredients into blades with rubber spatula as needed to keep ingredients moving (Fig. 2). With experience you will find you can remove cover and, with motor running, carefully move a narrow rubber spatula up and down tight against side of the container, **just** until whirlpool action starts.

14. Try processing heavy mixtures at low speeds. If motor labors, switch to a higher speed.

Figure 2

Special Blender Features

CYCLO-MATIC OPERATION—Blenders with a cycle-counter provide the homemaker with more control in the use of the blender. The cycle-counter turns the motor on for about two seconds and off for about two seconds automatically, this is one complete cycle. During the "off" period food is redistributed around the blades to make for more uniform processing. The instruction booklet provided by the manufacturer should be read carefully. Try a few family-favorite recipes to adjust to the timing in cycles required for different types and quantities of food being processed.

SOLID STATE—Blenders with solid state controls make blending possible at low speeds. This feature on a blender makes it possible to whip, stir, cream etc. at low speeds. High speeds on a blender have never been a problem. Solid State permits low speeds with power and it is probably the one single feature which has added a wide range of functions to the blender.

INFINITE SPEEDS—An infinite speed control on a blender offers limitless speeds from LO to HI. There are a number of positive speed positions marked on the nameplate and between each of these there is an infinite number of speeds. This feature permits you to select any speed from the LO to the HI range by the twist of a dial.

TIMERS—Blender timers are a convenience when blending foods which require careful timing. Just set the desired speed and blending time, the blender operates for the time period selected and automatically shuts itself off.

TOUCH 'N GO—This feature permits instant "On" and "Off" operation of the blender to obtain better distribution of food around the cutting blades. Thus you achieve quicker and more efficient blending. (See pages 10 and 11)

Blender Uses

FROZEN FRUIT JUICES AND FRUIT-ADES — There's little waiting when preparing frozen concentrated fruit juices or fruit-ades (Fig. 3). See Fast Fix Juices (page 21) for complete directions.

FROZEN CONCENTRATED SOUPS—See page 100 for complete directions.

QUICK CHILLED DRINKS—Iced tea, coffee, fruit drinks or ice water can be chilled in seconds, in the blender (Fig. 4). For short drinks have at least one cup of liquid in container. Add two or three ice cubes or ½ cup of crushed ice set speed at **STIR** (**2**) for 8 to 10 seconds. Strain ice or serve with crushed ice if preferred. When mixing several drinks at one time put 2 or more cups of liquid in container; set at **STIR** (**2**) and add 2 or more cups of ice cubes, one at a time, to container. Strain ice or serve with crushed ice if preferred.

When crushing ice have at least 2 cups of cold water in the container before adding the ice or ice cubes. Very cold or very large ice cubes are harder and therefore take longer to crush. Set speed at **GRATE** (**6**) for 8 to 10 seconds until ice is finely crushed.

This water chop method of crushing ice results in an ice slush. The ice must be strained to remove excess water. The remaining ice can then be used to chill beverages, make snow cones or slush cups etc. If you frequently use crushed ice an ice crusher attachment (see page 7) will be a handy item to add to your blender.

FROZEN FRUITS AND ICE CREAM OR SHERBET—Cut frozen fruits, very cold ice cream or sherbet into 1-inch cubes or chunks and follow directions for specific food being prepared.

Figure 3 *Figure 4*

Ice Crusher Attachment

Many blenders have separate ice crusher attachments that can give quantities of chipped ice in minutes. Some attachments have a Coarse-Medium-Fine Selector which gives a selection of ice chip size. Fine ice for frappés, cold drinks and snow cones; Medium for chilling appetizers, relishes and butter; Coarse for cooling bottled beverages and foods. Use of chipped ice for bumps, bruises, sponging and burn treatment in the home is recommended. Ice applied immediately to the burn area reduces the surface temperature and arrests the cooking of flesh. This minimizes the tissue damage, irritation and especially reduces pain. For serious burns seek immediate medical assistance. The above are only a few of the hundreds of valuable uses for ice and crushed ice.

BREAD CRUMBS—Beautiful Soft or Dry Bread Crumbs (see page 100).

CEREAL CRUMBS — Measure corn, bran or whole wheat flakes into container ½ cup at a time:

Figure 6

COARSE CRUMBS — For toppings, meat loaves or coating meats, chicken or croquettes. Set speed at **CRUMB** (**3**) then switch motor on and off until crumbs are desired fineness, 3 to 4 times. Yield: About 1 cup flakes makes ½ cup coarse crumbs.

FINE CRUMBS—For pie crust, cookies, etc. (Fig. 6). Proceed as for coarse crumbs except set speed at **CHOP** (**8**); process until crumbs are desired fineness, about 10 seconds. Yield: About 2 cups flakes makes ½ cup crumbs.

COOKIE CRUMBS — Break vanilla or chocolate wafers, brown edge or rich cookies or gingersnaps in half. Add 4 to 8 cookies to container at a time. Set speed at **HI** (**13**); switch motor on and off until crumbs are fineness desired, 10 to 14 times. Repeat as necessary. Yield: About 16 small or 10 large cookies makes about ½ cup crumbs.

CRACKER CRUMBS — Proceed as for cookie crumbs for small rich or soda crackers, graham crackers or sea toast, except break large crackers into quarters; set speed at **PUREE** (**4**). Process 4 small or 3 large crackers at a time to fineness desired, 6 to 8 times. Yield: About 16 small or 10 large crackers makes about ½ cup crumbs.

BLEND 'N STORE CONTAINERS—Most blender containers that have a detachable processing assembly are threaded to fit small or large mouth Mini or Blend 'N Store containers for food processing and storing. A small container is especially good for preparing baby and geriatric foods (Fig. 7), salad dressings, sandwich spreads, chopping nuts, grinding coffee beans and processing small quantities of food. When assembling the container for use, place the ingredients in the jar first and then the liquid or the most fluid mixture. Tempered Mini or Blend 'N Store containers can be used for freezing if the container is not filled more than ¾ full, allowing for space to expand. If mason or ordinary glass jars are used inspect them before using to be sure they are not chipped or cracked; do not use jars that are in any way defective. Do not process any hard substance such as ice cubes, hard candies, etc., which might chip or crack the jar. Excessively hot or cold jars must stand for 15 minutes before using to prevent breakage.

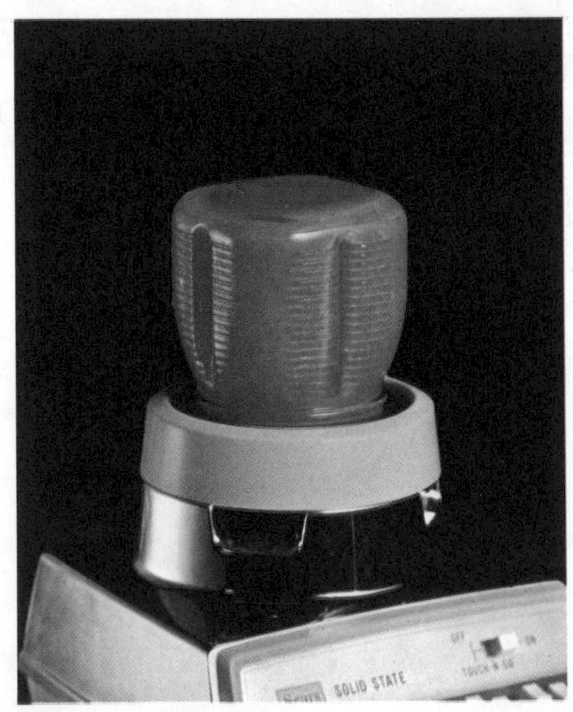

Figure 7

Figure 8

GRATING CHEESE—Blender grating of cheese (Fig. 8) is a time saver as well as being economical for left over or whole packaged cheese. Put about ½ cup cheese (cut in ½ inch cubes) in blender container or mini jar. Set speed at **GRATE (6)** and process about 15 seconds for moderately fine grated cheese. Repeat as needed. Cheese that is well chilled will grate best in the blender. See (page 100) for complete directions on the various types of cheese and the yield.

WATER-CHOP VEGETABLES (Fig. 9)—Cut raw carrots, cabbage, onions, red and green peppers, etc., into 1-inch pieces. Loosely fill container ⅔ full of vegetables. Cover vegetables with cold water. Cover container; turn speed to **CHOP (8)**; let motor run just until vegetables at top have traveled down to blades. Stop motor; empty container into colander or strainer; drain well. Repeat as needed. This method is especially good for processing large amounts of vegetables.

Dry-Chopped Fruits and Vegetables—Slice or dice fruit, raw or cooked vegetables into ¾ to 1-inch pieces and place in container. Process ½ to 1 cup at a time. Set speed at **LO (1)**, **STIR (2)** or **CRUMB (3)**. Tough vegetables, like carrots, chop best at **GRATE (6)**. The more tender the food the lower the speed. Switch motor on and off quickly until food particles are the desired size. Push ingredients into blades, as needed, with rubber spatula while motor is stopped. Repeat as necessary.

DRY-CHOP CELERY AND CARROTS—Chop 1 cup at a time. Cut celery in ¾-inch lengths and **CRUMB (3)**, Carrots in 1-inch peeled slices and **GRATE (6)**, as directed for Dry-Chopped Fruits and Vegetables. Yield about ½ cup.

DRY-CHOPPED ONION—Chop 1 medium onion (Fig. 10), quartered, at LO (1) as directed for Dry-Chopped Fruits and Vegetables. Yield about ½ cup.

CHOPPED CANDY—Candy canes, stick candy, chocolate covered toffee bars, peanut brittle and mints chop quickly in the blender. Chop a small amount of candy lengths (½ or 1-inch) or pieces at a time. Add candy to container; set speed at **STIR (2)**; switch motor on and off as needed to chop to fineness desired. Empty container; repeat as necessary.

Figure 9

Figure 10

Touch 'N Go

OZS
40
36
32
28
24
20
16
OFF
ON
TOUCH-N-GO
Sears
SOLID STATE
10 Speed Blender

Blender Basics

HOW TO CLEAN—Take care of your blender for long years of service.

Container—For a quick cleaning, pour a small amount of detergent into container (Fig. 12). Fill with warm water to 3 or 4-cup level. Cover. Turn speed to **LO** (**1**). Run motor 3 to 5 seconds or until food is loosened from container. Turn motor off; rinse well and dry carefully. On blender containers with removable processing assemblies (Fig. 13), remove parts, rinse well and dry carefully. Do not soak processing assembly for prolonged periods.

Base—Remove cord from electric outlet. Wipe cord with damp cloth; dry and push cord into storage area in base if provided. Wipe base carefully with damp cloth and dry well.

Figure 12

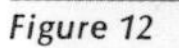

TOUCH 'N GO FEATURE—See photo at left. This is probably one of the best features engineered into the modern blender. It is especially good when working with foods that require a short blending time or with small quantities of food. For touch 'n go operation follow specific instructions provided by the manufacturer of your blender. Set at desired speed and momentarily activate switch as often as required.

Figure 13

Deviled Eggs

See photo at right

6 hard-cooked eggs
3 tablespoons Blender-Made Mayonnaise (page 79)
2 tablespoons Basic French Dressing (page 80)
2 teaspoons prepared mustard
¼ teaspoon salt
2 dashes Tabasco sauce

Cut eggs in half lengthwise. Remove yolks; save whites. **CRUMB (3)** egg yolks and remaining ingredients 10 seconds, or until smooth. Stop motor; push ingredients into blades with rubber spatula, as necessary. Refill whites with egg yolk mixture. If desired, garnish tops with bits of pimiento and thin black olive slices. Yield: 12 deviled eggs (halves).

DEVILED HAM 'N EGGS—Follow recipe for Deviled Eggs; stir **¼ cup finely chopped ham** into egg yolk mixture.

Bacon Cheese Tarts

See photo at right

1 cup coarsely chopped onion
½ cup half and half (or half milk half cream)
2 eggs
¼ pound Swiss or American cheese, cubed
1 teaspoon Worcestershire sauce
1 teaspoon prepared mustard
¼ teaspoon salt
⅛ teaspoon pepper
4 drops Tabasco sauce
8 slices crisp bacon, crumbled
*24 small, unbaked tart shells, 2½ inch diameter**

PUREE (4) onions until finely chopped, 2 to 3 seconds. Pour into bowl. Combine next 8 ingredients in blender container; **PUREE (4)** 5 seconds. Add bacon; **PUREE (4)** 5 seconds. Pour over onions; mix. Place pastry lined tart pans on baking sheet. Bake shells in moderate oven (375°F.) 10 minutes. Spoon filling into tart shells filling to within ⅛ inch from top. Return to oven; bake until filling is set, about 15 minutes. Yield: 24 tarts.

*If no tiny tart shells are available use small (2½-inch diameter) muffin pans, covering bottom and ½ inch up sides of each cup with pastry.

Appetizers

Roquefort or Blue Cheese Dip

2 packages (3 ounces each) room temperature cream cheese, cubed
½ cup Blender-Made Mayonnaise (page 79)
3 tablespoons cream or white wine
1 thin slice onion
1 teaspoon Worcestershire sauce
6 ounces Roquefort or blue cheese, crumbled (1 cup)

BLEND (10) all ingredients 15 seconds. Stop motor. Push ingredients into blades. Repeat as needed until smooth. Yield: About 2 cups.

Liver Sausage Pâté

See photo at right

⅓ cup Blender-Made Mayonnaise (page 79)
1 small (3-inch) dill pickle, sliced
1 5-inch green onion, in 1-inch slices
1 pound liver sausage, sliced
3 drops Tabasco sauce
1 package (8 ounce) room temperature cream cheese, optional
1½ cups coarsely chopped peanuts, pecans or walnuts (see page 100)

BLEND (10) first 5 ingredients 15 seconds; stop motor. Push ingredients into blades. Repeat process as needed until smooth. Pack into 1 pint bowl lined with plastic film. Chill until set. Turn onto plate. Remove plastic. Frost outside of ball, if desired, with cream cheese; coat with nuts. Yield: About 3⅔ cups if frosted, 2⅔ cups unfrosted.

Guacamole

See photo at right

2 medium avocados, peeled and cubed
1 medium tomato, quartered
1 (5-inch) green onion, in 1-inch slices
2 tablespoons lemon juice
½ teaspoon salt
2 dashes Tabasco sauce
2 canned green chili peppers, optional

CHOP (8) all ingredients 15 seconds; stop motor. Push ingredients into blades. Repeat process until smooth. Garnish with thin avocado slices and tomato wedges. Serve with corn chips. Yield: About 2¼ cups.

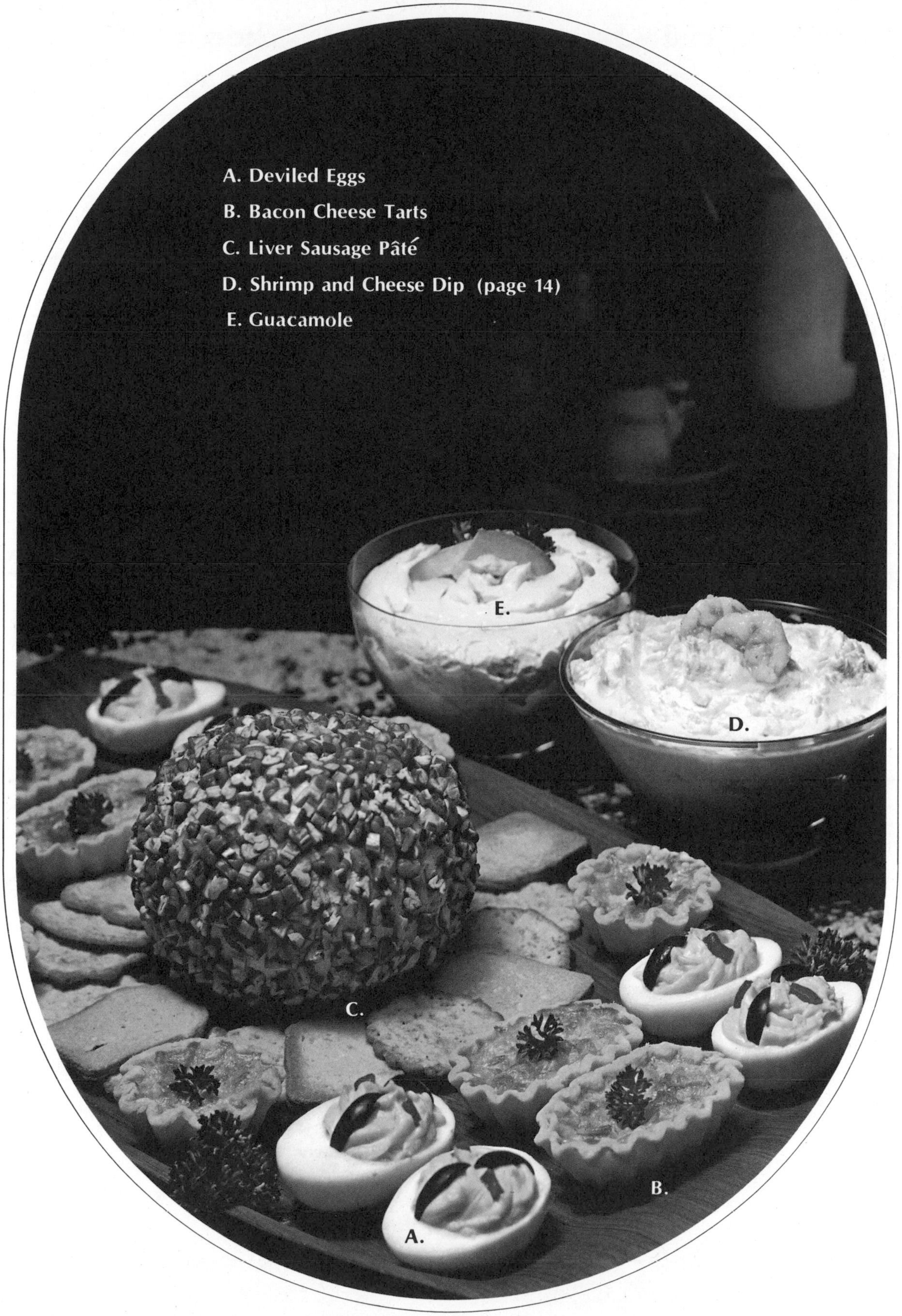

A. Deviled Eggs
B. Bacon Cheese Tarts
C. Liver Sausage Pâté
D. Shrimp and Cheese Dip (page 14)
E. Guacamole

Shrimp and Cheese Dip

See photo on page 13

1 package (8 ounce) room temperature cream cheese, cubed
1 can (4½ ounces) deveined shrimp, drained
½-inch square lemon rind
1 cup dairy sour cream
⅓ cup chutney
½ teaspoon curry powder

CHOP (8) all ingredients 15 seconds; stop motor. Push ingredients into blades. Repeat process as needed until smooth. Yield: About 2⅔ cups.

Smoked Fish Sour Cream Dip

½ cup dairy sour cream
⅛-inch unpeeled lemon slice, cut into quarters
1 thin slice onion
¼ teaspoon salt
¼ teaspoon rosemary, optional
4 sprigs parsley (no stems)
1 package (8 ounce) room temperature cream cheese, cubed
½ pound smoked fish (whitefish, chubs or other smoked fish) skinned, boned and flaked

STIR (2) first 6 ingredients just until well mixed, 2 to 3 seconds. Add ½ of cheese and **GRATE (6)** just until smooth, 4 to 5 seconds. Add remaining cheese; **GRATE (6)** just until mixed, 4 to 5 seconds. Stop motor and push ingredients into blades with rubber spatula, as needed. Turn into bowl and fold in flaked fish. Chill. Pile into serving dish and garnish, if desired, with a sprig of watercress or parsley. Serve with chips, thinly sliced fresh vegetables or crackers. Yield: About 2 cups.

Hot Bean and Bacon Dip

1 can (1 pound) pork and beans in tomato sauce
1 cup shredded sharp process American cheese
1 sliver garlic
1½ teaspoons chili powder
¼ teaspoon liquid smoke, optional
8 slices crisp bacon, in 1-inch pieces

GRATE (6) beans, ¾ cup cheese and seasonings 30 seconds. Stop motor; push ingredients into blades with rubber spatula, as necessary. Add bacon; **GRATE (6)** 20 seconds. Stop motor; push ingredients into blades, as necessary. Heat in chafing dish; top with remaining cheese. Serve with potato or corn chips. Yield: 2⅓ cups.

Cheese Spread Base

3 tablespoons half and half (or half milk half cream) or dairy sour cream
1 package (8 ounces) room temperature cream cheese, cubed
½ teaspoon seasoned salt
1 thin slice onion
½ teaspoon prepared mustard
Dash of pepper

Combine half and half or sour cream, ½ of the cream cheese and remaining ingredients in container. **MIX (7)** until smooth, 4 to 5 seconds. Add remaining cheese; **MIX (7)** until smooth, 4 to 5 seconds. Stop motor and push ingredients into blades with rubber spatula, as needed. Chill and use for making canapés and appetizers. Yield: About 1 cup.

SALAMI OR BOLOGNA CORNUCOPIAS—Select **salami, bologna** or other large fully cooked sausage. Cut slices in half and spread tops with **Cheese Spread Base** (above) mixture. Roll up cornucopia-fashion; hold in place with wooden picks. Cover and chill until serving time.

SARDINE OR ANCHOVY FILLET SPREAD—Follow recipe for **Cheese Spread Base** (above). Add **6 to 8** (more if desired) well-drained **small sardines or anchovy fillets** to mixture with last half of cream cheese. Chill. Pile in serving dish; garnish top with a sardine or anchovy fillet and sprig of watercress or parsley. Yield: About 1 cup.

Deviled Ham Dip

2 cans (3 ounces each) deviled ham
3 tablespoons Blender-Made Mayonnaise (page 79)
½ teaspoon horseradish
½ teaspoon prepared mustard
1 package (3 ounce) room temperature cream cheese, cubed
12 small stuffed olives
2 hard-cooked eggs, sliced

GRATE (6) first 5 ingredients 25 seconds, or until smooth. Stop motor and push ingredients into blades with rubber spatula, as necessary. Add olives. **CRUMB (3)** 5 to 6 seconds, or until olives are coarsely chopped. Add eggs. **CRUMB (3)** 5 to 6 seconds, or until eggs are coarsely chopped. Yield: About 1⅔ cups.

Fondue Bourguignonne

2 pounds lean beef sirloin or tenderloin, cut 1 to 1½ inches thick
Cooking oil, peanut or vegetable
Bearnaise, barbecue or favorite meat sauces (pages 82, 83 and 84)
Assorted fresh vegetables (cauliflower and cucumber slices, cherry or sliced tomatoes and green pepper rings) or tossed salad

Cut beef into cubes. Fill electric or flame type fondue pot half full with oil. Preheat oil in electric pot to 365°F. and you are ready to cook. For flame type pot preheat oil on range to 365°F. then place on stand over canned heat or alcohol burner. Let guests cook the cubed beef on long insulated handle fondue forks in the hot oil about 1 to 2 minutes or to the doneness desired. Meat can be dipped into Bearnaise and other favorite meat sauces and eaten with bread. Serve with crisp fresh vegetables or tossed salad. For flame type pot reheat oil on range if needed to keep it sizzling hot. Yield: About 6 servings.

Hot Dog Sandwich Spread

Egg and Salami Sandwich Spread

Sausage-Cheese Burgers

Sandwich Fillings

Egg Salad Sandwich Filling

4 hard-cooked eggs, quartered
½ cup Blender-Made Mayonnaise (page 79)
1 3-inch sweet pickle, in ½-inch slices
½ teaspoon celery salt
½ teaspoon salt
Dash of pepper

Add 4 egg quarters, at a time, to container. Set speed at **STIR** (**2**) then switch motor on and off 2 times. Empty into mixing bowl. Repeat until all eggs are chopped. Combine remaining ingredients in container. **CHOP** (**8**) until pickles are coarsely chopped, 3 to 5 seconds. Add to eggs; mix by hand. Yield: About 1⅔ cups; filling for about 6 to 8 sandwiches.

EGG AND SALAMI SANDWICH SPREAD—(See photo at left)—Prepare one recipe of **Egg Salad Sandwich Filling** (above). Dice **6 slices of hard or cotto salami** and **2 tablespoons each of pimiento and green pepper.** Fold into egg salad. Yield: About 2 cups filling.

Hot Dog Sandwich Spread

See photo at left

1 cup ½-inch fully-cooked frankfurter or wiener slices (about 4)
½ cup Blender-Made Mayonnaise (page 79)
2 2-inch sweet pickles, in 1-inch slices
1 thin slice small onion

Place ¼ cup of sausage slices in container. Set speed at **STIR** (**2**) then switch motor on and off until meat is coarsely chopped, 4 or 5 times. Empty into small mixing bowl; repeat 3 times. Add remaining ingredients to container; **STIR** (**2**) until pickles are coarsely chopped, 4 to 5 seconds. Add to chopped meat and mix. Yield: About 1⅓ cups, filling for 5 to 6 sandwiches.

Cheese Spread

2 cups diced (½-inch) chilled Cheddar cheese
⅓ cup Blender-Made Mayonnaise (page 79)
1 5-inch green onion, in 1-inch slices
2 teaspoons prepared mustard

GRATE (6) cheese, ½ cup at a time, until coarsely chopped, about 8 seconds each time. Empty into bowl. Combine remaining ingredients in container. **GRATE (6)** until onion is coarsely chopped and stir into cheese. Use for making hot or cold cheese sandwiches. Yield: About 1½ cups.

Sausage-Cheese Burgers

See photo at left

6 buttered sandwich buns
12 slices cotto salami, bologna or New England brand sausage
½ recipe Cheese Spread (above)

Cover bottom halves of buns with ½ of sausage slices; spread each with an equal amount of cheese mixture and top with a sausage slice. Arrange on baking sheet with bun tops, cut side up. Heat in broiler, 4 to 5 inches from heat source until sausage heats and cheese softens, 3 to 5 minutes. Cover with bun tops and serve. Yield: 6 sandwiches.

Baked Denver Sandwiches

6 eggs
¼ green pepper, cut into 1-inch squares
½ small onion, sliced
½ teaspoon salt
¼ teaspoon pepper
1 cup diced fully-cooked ham
12 buttered toast slices

Combine first 5 ingredients in container. **STIR (2)** until peppers are coarsely chopped, 3 to 5 seconds. Add ham; **STIR (2)** just until ham is coarsely chopped, 4 to 6 seconds. Pour into well buttered 13 x 9 x 2 inch baking dish. Bake in moderate oven (375°F.) until egg is cooked, about 10 minutes. Cut into six servings. Place each on a toast slice and top with second toast slice. Yield: 6 sandwiches.

Salmon Salad Sandwich Filling

⅔ cup Blender-Made Mayonnaise (page 79)
2 tablespoons Basic French Dressing (page 80)
1 thin slice unpeeled lemon, quartered
1 thin small onion slice
½ teaspoon salt
½ teaspoon celery salt
2 3-inch sweet pickles, in ½ inch slices
1 can (1 pound) salmon drained, skinned, boned and flaked
⅓ cup diced celery

Combine first 6 ingredients in container; **STIR (2)** just until lemon and onion are finely chopped, about 5 seconds. Add pickles; **STIR (2)** just until pickles are coarsely chopped. Turn into bowl; fold in salmon and celery by hand. Yield: About 2¼ cups; filling for about 8 sandwiches.

Peanut Butter Spread

2 tablespoons melted butter or margarine
1 tablespoon cooking oil
1 can (6¾ ounces) salted peanuts (about 1⅓ cups)

Combine ingredients in container. **BLEND (10)** 15 seconds. Stop motor and push ingredients into blades with rubber spatula, as needed. Repeat process as many times as needed for a chunky or smooth consistency. Yield: About ¾ cup.

Chicken or Turkey Pecan Sandwich Spread

½ cup Blender-Made Mayonnaise (page 79)
½ cup pecan halves
½ teaspoon celery salt
½ teaspoon salt
1 cup diced cooked chicken or turkey
⅓ cup diced celery

Combine first 4 ingredients in container. **STIR (2)** just until pecans are coarsely chopped. Add chicken or turkey; set speed at **STIR (2)** then switch motor on and off until poultry is chopped medium fine. Empty into bowl; fold in celery by hand. Yield: About 1¾ cups, filling for 5 to 6 sandwiches.

Cheese-Sausage Sandwich Loaf

See photo below

2 cups diced (½-inch) chilled Cheddar cheese (about 8 to 10 ounces)
4 5-inch green onions, in 1-inch slices
¼ medium green pepper, diced
¼ cup Blender-Made Mayonnaise (page 79)
1 tablespoon prepared mustard
1 loaf Vienna bread (12 to 13 inch)
8 to 12 slices bologna or other favorite cold cuts

GRATE (**6**) cheese, ½ cup at a time, until coarsely chopped, about 8 seconds each time. Pour into mixing bowl. **GRATE** (**6**) onions and green pepper until coarsely chopped, about 5 seconds and add to cheese. Stir in mayonnaise and mustard. Cut bread crosswise, not quite through bottom crust, into ½ or ¾-inch slices. Spread cut surfaces of every other slit with cheese mixture and insert a folded slice of bologna or other cold cut in each. Wrap loaf in aluminum foil. Bake in hot oven (400°F.) until hot, about 20 minutes or place to one side on grids of a charcoal grill. Allow bread to heat and cheese to melt. To serve, cut through bottom crust on either side of filled sections to form a sandwich. Yield: One loaf, about 8 to 12 servings.

CHICKEN, TURKEY OR HAM SALAD FOR SANDWICHES—See Chicken, Turkey or Ham Salad recipe, page 76).

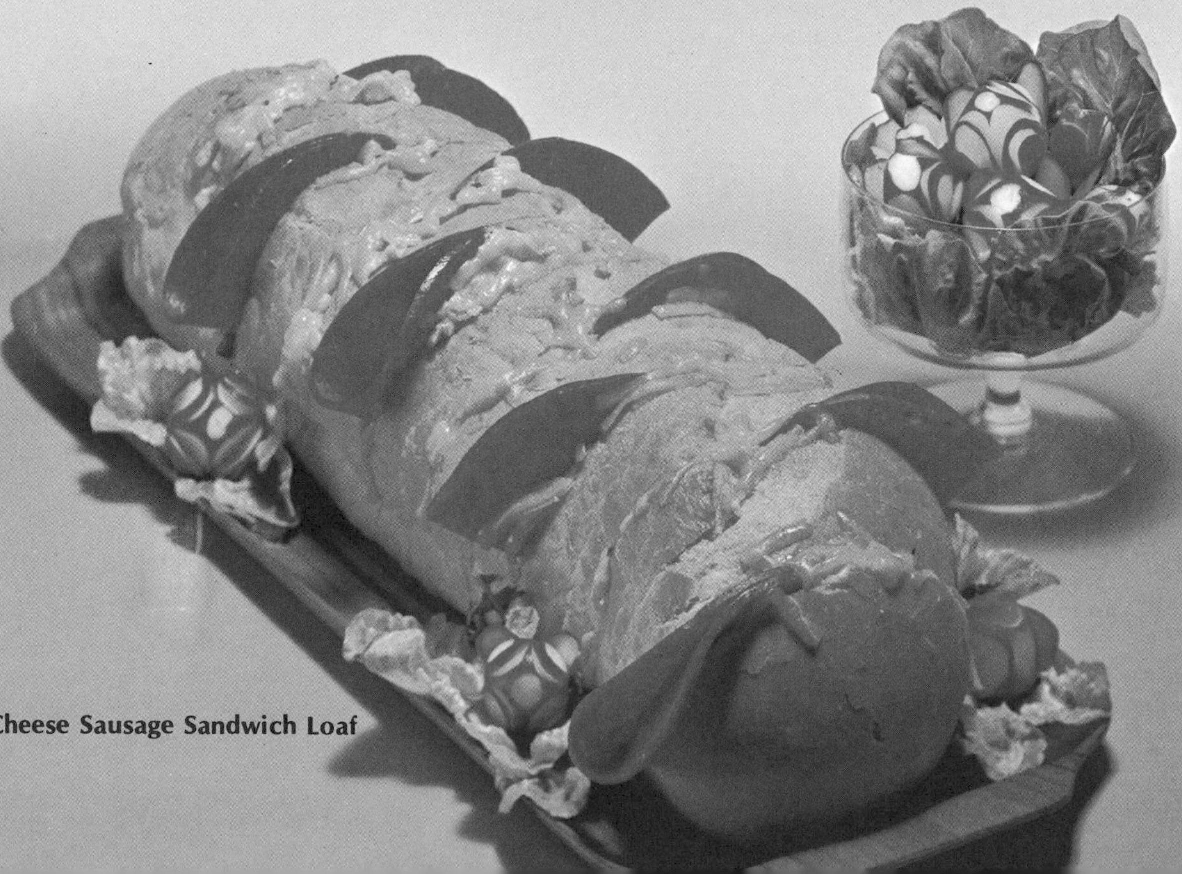

Cheese Sausage Sandwich Loaf

Smoked Sausage Sandwich Pizza

See photo below

½ cup milk
1 thin slice onion
2 cups prepared biscuit mix
½ teaspoon dry mustard
½ teaspoon fines herbes blend, optional
3 cups Sausage Sandwich Filling (below)
2 small tomatoes, cut in eighths
4 fully-cooked smoked sausage links, cut in half lengthwise and crosswise

CRUMB (**3**) milk and onion 3 to 4 seconds, or until onion is finely chopped. Add to biscuit mix, mustard and fines herbes blend, if used. Stir to make soft dough; turn onto lightly floured board and knead 10 to 12 strokes. Roll to fit bottom of well buttered 12-inch pizza pan. Bake in hot oven (400°F.) until done and lightly browned, about 10 minutes. Cool. Spread sausage filling evenly over crust. Alternate tomato wedges and sausage pieces, cut ends toward center, around outside edge of crust. To serve, cut in wedges. Yield: About 8 to 10 servings.

SAUSAGE SANDWICH FILLING—Follow recipe for Chicken, Turkey or Ham Salad (page 76) and substitute chopped **smoked sausage links** for poultry or ham.

Smoked Sausage Sandwich Pizza

Frosty Fruit Sparkler
(page 22)

Grape Float
(page 22)

Lemon or Limeade
(page 23)

Mexican Cocoa

Strawberry Buttermilk Whirl
(page 23)

Fast Fix Juices

Beverages

The modern blender mixes plain or fancy drinks in seconds. All of the favorites—the thick malts, shakes, smoothies, floats, fruit and milk drinks and hot beverages, as well as ice tinkling refreshers for the elders. Use your own recipes or any of the following.

These few guides guarantee success.

1. Don't overload the container. Prepare the recipe as many times as needed, it takes only a jiffy.
2. Use low speeds for all heavy mixtures.
3. When needed, stop motor and push ingredients into blades with rubber spatula.
4. Don't overblend! The time given in the recipes is just a guide. Remember it takes just seconds to mix most beverages. Stop the motor the instant the desired consistency is obtained.
5. To chill beverages quickly add cracked or crushed ice or ice cubes, one at a time.
6. It's safe to pour hot (scalded) milk or water into most containers.
7. Chocolate need not be melted when hot milk or water is used.
8. Ice cream or sherbet should be cubed or scooped before adding to container. For thick ice cream drinks shorten blending time.
9. Fresh fruits should be cleaned, cubed and seeded and any coarse rind or fiber removed before using.
10. Carbonated beverages should be stirred into drinks gently, by hand, just before serving.

Fast Fix Juices

See photo at left

Empty **1 can (6 ounces) frozen fruit juice concentrate** (orange, lemonade, tangerine, grape, boysenberry etc.,) into container. Add the amount of cold water recommended on label. **STIR (2)** until well mixed, 4 to 5 seconds. Yield: About 3 cups.

Hot Cocoa

2 cups hot (scalded) milk
2 or 3 tablespoons cocoa
¼ cup sugar
½ teaspoon vanilla
Dash of salt
Whipped cream or marshmallows, optional

STIR (2) all ingredients 5 seconds. Garnish servings with whipped cream or marshmallows, if desired. Yield: About 2¼ cups, 2 to 3 servings.

Mexican Cocoa

See photo at left

Follow recipe for Hot Cocoa (above) and add ¼ **to** ½ **teaspoon cinnamon** before blending. **STIR (2)** 5 seconds. Garnish each serving with whipped cream and a **cinnamon stick.** Yield: About 2¼ cups, 2 to 3 servings.

Thick Malts

1½ cups chilled milk
4 tablespoons malted-milk powder
1 teaspoon vanilla
1 pint vanilla ice cream, cubed

CRUMB (3) first 3 ingredients and ½ of the ice cream 8 to 10 seconds or until thick and smooth. Stop motor, push ingredients into blades, if necessary. Add remaining ice cream; **CRUMB (3)** just until ice cream is mixed in, about 8 seconds. Yield: About 3½ cups, 2 to 4 servings.

Thick Chocolate Malts

Follow recipe for Thick Malts and use **chocolate-flavored** instead of plain **malted-milk powder** and add ⅓ **cup chocolate syrup** with milk. Chocolate ice cream may be used instead of vanilla, if desired.

Strawberry Malts

Follow recipe for Thick Malts and add **2 to 3 tablespoonfuls of strawberry syrup** or ½ **cup defrosted frozen sweetened strawberries** with the milk.

Orange Buttermilk Punch

Orange Buttermilk Punch

See photo at left

2 cups chilled buttermilk
½ of 6 ounce can frozen orange juice concentrate, partially defrosted
1 pint vanilla ice cream, cubed
Orange slices and mint sprigs, optional

CRUMB (3) first 2 ingredients and ½ pint ice cream, 5 seconds. Pour into chilled punch bowl; spoon additional ½ pint vanilla ice cream over punch. Garnish punch with half orange slices and mint sprigs, if desired. Prepare as many individual batches of punch as needed before topping with ice cream and garnishing. Yield: About 4 cups, 8 servings.

Frosty Fruit Sparkler

See photo page 20

4 small or 3 large, drained, canned peach halves
¼-inch slice unpeeled lime, quartered
½ cup cold water
⅓ cup frozen orange juice concentrate, defrosted
2 tablespoons sugar
1 cup cracked ice
2 bottles (10 ounces each) chilled gingerale
Orange slices or mint sprigs, optional

CRUMB (3) first 6 ingredients, 20 seconds, or until ice melts. Pour an equal amount of mixture into 4 tall glasses over 2 ice cubes; fill with gingerale. Stir gently. Garnish glasses, if desired, with orange slices and mint sprigs. Yield: About 4½ cups, 4 servings.

Grape Float

See photo page 20

1 can (6 ounce) frozen grape juice concentrate, partially defrosted
½ cup cold water
2 pints vanilla ice cream or pineapple sherbet, cubed
2 bottles (10 ounces each) chilled gingerale

BLEND (10) grape juice, water and 1 pint ice cream or sherbet, about 10 seconds, or until evenly mixed. Pour an equal amount into 6 tall glasses and add gingerale. Stir gently. Spoon remaining ice cream or sherbet into glass. Yield: About 6 cups; 6 large servings.

Lemon or Limeade

See photo page 20

½ inch square lemon or lime rind
½ cup lemon or lime juice
½ cup sugar
2 cups cold water
1 cup crushed ice
Lime or lemon slices, optional
Maraschino cherries and mint sprigs, optional

GRATE (6) first 5 ingredients 15 seconds, or until well mixed. Pour over additional crushed ice. Garnish with lime or lemon slices, maraschino cherry and mint, as desired. Yield: About 3¼ cups, 4 servings.

Strawberry Buttermilk Whirl

See photo page 20

2 cups chilled buttermilk
1 package (10 ounce) frozen strawberries, partially defrosted and cubed
2 drops red food color
2 tablespoons sugar
1 pint strawberry ice cream, cubed
Mint sprigs, optional

GRATE (6) first 4 ingredients, 15 seconds, or until well mixed. Pour into 4 tall glasses; top each with a scoop of ice cream and if desired, garnish with mint. Yield: About 5 cups, 4 tall drinks.

Strawberry Shake

See photo at right

Follow recipe for **Strawberry Buttermilk Whirl** (above) and substitute **chilled whole milk** for the buttermilk. Yield: about 5 cups, 4 tall drinks.

Strawberry Shake

Speedy Hot Chocolate

½ cup semi-sweet chocolate bits
3 tablespoons sugar
3 cups hot (scalded) milk
1 teaspoon vanilla
Whipped cream or marshmallows, optional

GRATE (**6**) first 2 ingredients and ½ cup hot milk 5 seconds, or until chocolate melts. Stop motor. Add remaining milk and vanilla; **STIR** (**2**) 5 seconds. Top each serving with whipped cream or marshmallows, if desired. Yield: About 3¼ cups, 4 to 5 servings.

Strawberry Milk Cooler

1 package (10 ounce) frozen strawberries, partially defrosted and cubed
2 tablespoons sugar
4 cups chilled milk

CRUMB (**3**) strawberries, sugar and 2 cups milk 10 to 15 seconds or until strawberries are finely chopped. Pour into serving pitcher and stir in remaining milk. Yield: About 5 cups, 4 servings.

Raspberry Milk Cooler

Follow recipe for Strawberry Milk Cooler and substitute **frozen raspberries** for strawberries.

Grape Chiller

1 can (6 ounce) frozen grape juice concentrate, partially defrosted
½ of 6 ounce can frozen orange juice concentrate, partially defrosted
2 thin unpeeled lime or lemon slices, quartered
1½ cups cold water
1 cup crushed ice
2 bottles (10 ounces each) chilled gingerale

CRUMB (**3**) first 5 ingredients 20 seconds, or until lime or lemon is finely chopped. Pour an equal amount of mixture into 6 tall glasses over ice cubes; fill glasses with gingerale and stir gently. Yield: About 6 cups, 6 servings.

Cafe-au-Lait Shake

2 cups chilled milk
1 tablespoon instant coffee
1 tablespoon sugar
2 pints coffee or vanilla ice cream, cubed
Whipped cream, optional

CRUMB (**3**) first 3 ingredients and 1 pint ice cream 5 seconds, or until smooth. Pour into tall glasses. Top with remaining ice cream and if desired, garnish with whipped cream. Yield: About 5½ cups, 4 to 6 servings.

Eggnogs

See recipes page 95

Chocolate Mint Shake

2 cups chilled half and half (half milk half cream) or undiluted evaporated milk
½ cup chocolate syrup
3 tablespoons sugar
1 teaspoon vanilla
⅛ teaspoon peppermint extract
1 cup crushed ice
1 pint peppermint ice cream and mint sprigs, optional

STIR (**2**) first 6 ingredients 5 seconds, or until well mixed. Pour into 4 to 6 tall glasses. Top with ice cream and mint sprigs, if desired. Yield: About 3½ cups without ice cream or 5½ cups with ice cream, 4 to 6 servings.

Quick-Do Lemonade or Limeade

1 can (6 ounce) frozen lemonade or limeade concentrate, partially defrosted
2 cups cold water
1½ cups crushed ice
Yellow or green food color, optional
Lemon or lime slices or mint sprigs, optional

STIR (**2**) first 3 ingredients 10 seconds, or until well mixed. Tint a pale yellow or green with food color, if desired. To serve, pour over additional crushed ice. Garnish glasses with lemon or lime slices and mint sprigs. Yield: About 3¾ cups, 4 to 6 servings.

Liquid Measuring Guide

1 jigger = 3 tablespoons or 1½ ounces
1 ounce = 2 tablespoons
4 ounces = ½ measuring cup or 8 tablespoons
8 ounces = 1 measuring cup or 16 tablespoons
Juice of 1 lemon = about 3 tablespoons
Juice of 1 lime = about 1½ tablespoons

Alexander

See photo page 27

4 jiggers gin
4 jiggers crème de cacao
4 jiggers whipping cream or half and half
1 cup cracked ice

Combine ingredients in container; turn to **LO** (**1**) for 2 to 3 seconds and strain. Yield: 4 servings.

Brandy Alexander

Follow recipe for Alexander; substitute **brandy** for gin.

Grasshopper

Follow recipe for Alexander; use **white crème de cacao** and substitute **crème de menthe** for gin.

Orange Blossom

4 jiggers light rum or gin
¾ cup orange juice
2 tablespoons lemon or lime juice
2 teaspoons sugar
1 cup cracked ice
Orange slices

STIR (**2**) first 5 ingredients 10 to 12 seconds or to consistency of sherbet. Garnish glasses with orange slices. Yield: 4 servings.

Pink Lady

See photo page 27

2 jiggers gin
1 jigger apple brandy
2 tablespoons lemon juice
2 tablespoons grenadine
2 egg whites
1 cup cracked ice

Combine ingredients in container; turn to **LO** (**1**) for 5 to 6 seconds; strain, if desired. Yield: 4 servings.

Bacardi Cocktail

See photo page 27

4 jiggers Bacardi rum
2 jiggers lime juice
1 teaspoon grenadine
2 teaspoons sugar
2 cups cracked ice

STIR (**2**) ingredients 10 to 12 seconds or to desired consistency. Yield: 4 servings.

Vodka Froth

2 jiggers vodka
1 cup grape juice
1 jigger lemon juice
1 egg white
1 cup cracked ice

STIR (**2**) ingredients 10 seconds or until smooth. Yield: 4 servings.

Bloody Mary

1 cup chilled tomato juice
6 jiggers vodka
⅓ cup lemon juice
4 dashes Worcestershire sauce
¼ teaspoon salt
1 cup cracked ice

CRUMB (**3**) ingredients 15 seconds or until ice melts. Yield: 4 servings.

Whiskey Sour

See photo at right

5 jiggers whiskey
¼ cup lemon juice
1 tablespoon fine granulated sugar
4 to 6 ice cubes
Orange slices and maraschino cherries

STIR (**2**) first 4 ingredients 8 to 10 seconds. Strain into glasses. Garnish with orange slice and maraschino cherry. Yield: 4 servings.

Frozen Daiquiri

2 jiggers light rum
2 tablespoons lime or lemon juice
1½ cups crushed ice
2 teaspoons confectioners' sugar

STIR (**2**) ingredients 10 to 12 seconds until slushy or of desired texture. Serve immediately. For sherbet-like consistency, reduce blending time. Serve in chilled champagne glasses with straws. Yield: 2 servings.

Mint Daiquiri

Follow recipe for Frozen Daiquiri. Add **2 to 4 fresh mint leaves** before blending.

Crème de Menthe Frappé

See photo at right

Pack well chilled glasses with well drained crushed ice (page 7). Drizzle crème de menthe over until glass is filled. Serve with straws.

Sloe Gin Fizz

See photo at right

2 jiggers lemon juice
1 tablespoon sugar
4 jiggers sloe gin
1 cup cracked ice
Chilled carbonated water
Mint sprigs, optional

STIR (**2**) first 4 ingredients 8 to 10 seconds. Strain into 4 10-ounce glasses over 1 or 2 ice cubes. Fill glasses with carbonated water; stir gently. Garnish with mint, if desired. Yield: 4 servings.

Gin Fizz

Follow directions for Sloe Gin Fizz; use **gin** instead of sloe gin.

Tom Collins

2 jiggers lemon or lime juice
2 jiggers gin
2 tablespoons sugar
1 cup cracked ice
Chilled carbonated water
Lemon or lime slices and maraschino cherries

STIR (**2**) first 4 ingredients 8 to 10 seconds. Strain an equal amount over ice cubes in 2 tall glasses. Fill glasses with carbonated water; stir gently. Garnish with lemon or lime slices and cherry. Yield: 2 tall drinks.

Mint Collins

Follow recipe for Tom Collins. Add **2 to 4 mint leaves** before blending.

Rum Collins

Follow recipe for Tom Collins; substitute **rum** for gin.

Crème de Menthe Frappé
Whiskey Sour
Pink Lady
Bacardi Cocktail
Sloe Gin Fizz
Alexander

Banana Bread
Fresh Apple Muffins

Breads

Fresh Apple Muffins

See photo at left

2 cups sifted flour
½ cup sugar
3 teaspoons baking powder
1 teaspoon pumpkin pie spice mix
¾ teaspoon salt
¼ cup melted shortening or cooking oil
2 eggs
⅓ cup milk
1½ cups coarsely chopped unpeeled apple

Sift first 5 ingredients into mixing bowl. **CRUMB** (**3**) shortening or oil, eggs, milk and apple in container 10 seconds or until apple is finely chopped. Pour over dry ingredients; stir just until dry ingredients are moistened. Fill greased, muffin pans (2½ x 1¼ inch) ¾ full. Bake in hot oven (400°F.) until done, about 20 minutes. Yield: 12 muffins.

Nut Bread

2 cups sifted flour
2 teaspoons baking powder
½ teaspoon salt
1 cup pecan halves
1¼ cups milk
1 teaspoon vanilla
2 eggs
⅓ cup soft shortening
1 cup sugar

Combine and sift first 3 ingredients into mixing bowl. Empty nuts into container. Set speed at **CHOP** (**8**) and turn switch on and off until nuts are coarsely chopped. Stir nuts into dry ingredients. **STIR** (**2**) milk, vanilla, eggs, shortening and sugar until well mixed, about 15 seconds. Pour into dry ingredients; mix just until dry ingredients are moistened. Spoon into well-greased, floured 9 x 5 x 3 inch loaf pan. Bake in moderate oven (350°F.) until done and lightly browned, 55 to 60 minutes. Yield: 9 x 5 x 2½ inch loaf.

Banana Bread

See photo at left

2½ cups sifted flour
⅔ cup sugar
3 teaspoons baking powder
1 teaspoon salt
½ teaspoon nutmeg
2 eggs
⅓ cup milk
⅓ cup melted shortening or cooking oil
1½ cups sliced banana (2 medium)
1 cup pecan halves

Sift first 5 ingredients into mixing bowl. **CRUMB** (**3**) eggs, milk, shortening or oil and bananas in container 5 seconds or until smooth. Add pecans; **CRUMB** (**3**) 3 to 4 seconds or until pecans are coarsely chopped. Pour over dry ingredients; mix just until dry ingredients are moistened. Pour into greased, floured loaf pan (9 x 5 x 3 inch). Bake in moderate oven (350°F.) until done, about 1 hour. Cool in pan 5 minutes; remove from pan and finish cooling on rack. Yield: One 9 x 5 x 3 inch loaf.

Popovers

2 eggs
1 cup milk
2 tablespoons melted butter or margarine
1 cup sifted flour
½ teaspoon salt

Combine ingredients in container in order listed. **MIX** (**7**) 25 to 30 seconds or until free of lumps. If necessary, stop motor and push ingredients into blades with rubber spatula. Fill well-greased 5-ounce custard cups or muffin pans ½ full. Bake in hot oven (400°F.) until brown and crisp, 35 to 40 minutes. If desired, batter may be prepared several hours before serving and refrigerated until baking time. About 5 minutes additional baking time will be needed for chilled batter. Yield: 8 large popovers.

Herb Popovers

Add ½ **teaspoon fines herbes blend** with dry ingredients when making **popovers** (above).

Quick Pancakes

Use a pancake mix. Follow package directions except combine liquids in container first then add package mix. **MIX** (7) 12 to 15 seconds or just until ingredients are mixed. Bake as directed on package.

Buttermilk Pancakes

2 eggs
1½ cups buttermilk
¼ cup melted shortening or cooking oil
3 tablespoons sugar
¾ teaspoon salt
1½ cups sifted flour
1½ teaspoons baking powder
1 teaspoon soda

Combine eggs, ¾ cup buttermilk and remaining ingredients in container. **MIX** (7) 30 seconds or just until ingredients are mixed. Stop motor; stir with rubber spatula and add remaining ¾ cup buttermilk. **MIX** (7) 20 seconds or until smooth. For each pancake pour ¼ cup batter onto hot lightly greased griddle. Turn pancakes when edges are dry and top full of bubbles; brown second side. Yield: About 3⅓ cups, 12 to 14 pancakes.

Thin Pancakes for Crêpes and Blintzes

1 cup sifted flour
1 teaspoon baking powder
1 tablespoon sugar
½ teaspoon salt
1 cup milk
2 eggs
1 teaspoon melted shortening or cooking oil

Sift first 4 ingredients onto waxed paper. Put remaining ingredients in container; **STIR** (2) until well mixed, 2 to 3 seconds. Add ½ of dry ingredients to container; **MIX** (7) until ingredients are mixed, about 10 seconds. Repeat using remaining dry ingredients. Pour 3 tablespoons batter into hot greased 6-inch fry pan; rotate pan quickly to spread batter evenly. Cook until cake is lightly browned; turn and brown second side. Stack cakes until all are cooked then make into Cheese Blintzes, (page 46) or Dessert Pancakes (page 45). Yield: About 12 thin pancakes.

Potato Pancakes

2 eggs
2 tablespoons milk
2 tablespoons melted butter or margarine
2 tablespoons flour
¾ teaspoon salt
⅛ teaspoon pepper
¼ small onion, sliced
2 cups peeled, diced raw potatoes.

MIX (7) first 7 ingredients and 1 cup potatoes 5 seconds. Add remaining 1 cup potatoes; **MIX** (7) 8 seconds or until coarsely chopped. For each pancake pour ¼ cup mixture onto hot, well-greased, griddle and spread into a 4-inch cake. Brown on first side; turn and brown on second side. Yield: About 2 cups, 8 pancakes.

Waffles

2 eggs, separated
1½ cups milk
¼ cup melted shortening or cooking oil
2 tablespoons sugar
¾ teaspoon salt
1½ cups sifted flour
2 teaspoons baking powder

Combine egg yolks and next 2 ingredients in container. **MIX** (7) 2 to 3 seconds. Add dry ingredients; **STIR** (2) just until mixed, 5 to 7 seconds. Do not overblend. Pour into mixing bowl; fold stiffly beaten egg whites into batter. Bake in preheated waffle iron. Yield: Three 9-inch square waffles.

Ham Waffles

Just before closing waffle iron sprinkle **2 tablespoons finely chopped cooked ham** over waffle batter (above). Serve waffles with syrup or for a luncheon dish top with creamed vegetables or favorite a la King mixture.

Pecan Waffles

Fold ½ cup coarsely chopped pecans (see page 100) into waffle batter (above) just before adding egg whites. Serve with syrup, or for a dessert, top waffles with ice cream and defrosted, frozen, sliced peaches or strawberries, or sundae sauce.

Quick-Made Muffins from a Mix

Follow package directions. Combine all but dry ingredients in container. **STIR** (**2**) until well mixed, 2 to 3 seconds. Stop motor; add dry ingredients. Mix slightly with rubber spatula. **STIR** (**2**) just until dry ingredients are moistened, 5 to 10 seconds. Stop motor and push ingredients into blades with rubber spatula as needed. Bake as directed on label.

Hi-Top Muffins

2 cups sifted flour
3 teaspoons baking powder
½ teaspoon salt
1 egg
1 cup milk
¼ cup melted shortening or cooking oil
¼ cup sugar

Sift first 3 ingredients into mixing bowl. **MIX** (**7**) remaining ingredients in container until well mixed, 5 to 10 seconds. Pour into dry ingredients; stir just until dry ingredients are moistened. Fill well-greased muffin pans ⅔ full. Bake in hot oven (400°F.) until done and lightly browned, about 25 minutes. Yield: About 12 muffins.

BLUEBERRY MUFFINS—Fold **1 cup fresh or well drained canned blueberries** into Quick-Made or Hi-Top batter (above) just before filling pans.

FRUITY MUFFINS—Fold **½ cup of seedless raisins, currants, chopped dates or apricots** into Quick-Made or Hi-Top batter (above) just before filling pans.

BACON MUFFINS—Fold **½ cup crisp bacon bits** into Quick-Made or Hi-Top batter (above) just before filling pans.

NUT MUFFINS—Fold **½ to ⅔ cup coarsely chopped pecans** (see page 100) into Quick-Made or Hi-Top batter (above) just before filling pans.

CORNMEAL MUFFINS—Substitute **1 cup yellow cornmeal** for 1 cup of flour in Hi-Top Recipe above. Substitute **bacon drippings** for shortening, if desired.

Yeast Bread

2 cups milk, scalded
2 packages active dry yeast
3 tablespoons sugar
2 tablespoons shortening
2 teaspoons salt
About 7 cups sifted flour

Cool milk to lukewarm and combine in container with next 4 ingredients; let stand 3 to 4 minutes. **WHIP** (**5**) until mixed, 5 to 8 seconds. Pour into large bowl. Stir in flour needed to make a dough which handles easily, adding ½ of flour at a time. Turn onto floured board; knead until smooth and elastic. Place in greased bowl; grease top. Cover; set in warm place (85°F.) until doubled in size. Punch dough down. Cut dough in half; shape each piece into a loaf. Place in greased 9 x 5 x 3 inch pans. Cover; set in warm place until doubled. Bake in moderate oven (375°F.) 45 to 50 minutes, or until done. Turn out of pans; cool on rack. Yield: 2 loaves.

RAISIN OR NUT BREAD—Follow Yeast Bread recipe; (above) increase sugar to ¼ cup. Stir in **1 cup seedless raisins** or **coarsely chopped nuts** after ½ of the flour has been added.

Graham Cracker Crumb Muffins

1 cup sifted flour
⅓ cup sugar
3 teaspoons baking powder
½ teaspoon salt
1 cup graham cracker crumbs
¼ cup cooking oil or melted shortening
1¼ cups milk
1 egg

Combine and sift first 4 ingredients into mixing bowl. Stir in graham cracker crumbs. Measure oil or shortening, milk and egg into contianer; **STIR** (**2**) until well mixed, about 10 seconds. Pour into dry ingredients and mix just until dry ingredients are moistened. Fill well-greased muffin pans ⅔ full. Bake in moderate oven (375°F.) until done and lightly browned, 18 to 20 minutes. Yield: About 12 muffins.

Cake Mixes

Use any prepared cake mix except angel food, sponge, chiffon or pound cake. Combine liquid and eggs called for on package label in container. Add ½ of cake mix. Stir with rubber spatula. **MIX** (7) 10 seconds. Stop motor. Add remaining cake mix. Scrape down sides of container and push ingredients into blades as necessary. **MIX** (7) 20 seconds; push ingredients into blades with rubber spatula. **MIX** (7) 10 seconds or until smooth. Bake as directed on package label.

Orange Cake

1⅓ cups orange juice
Rind of ½ medium orange, cut into 1-inch pieces
2 eggs
1 package (about 17 to 18 ounces) yellow cake mix

Combine orange juice, orange rind pieces, and eggs in container. Add one-half of cake mix. Stir with rubber spatula. **MIX** (**7**) 10 seconds. Stop motor. Add remaining cake mix. Scrape down sides of container and push ingredients into blades. **MIX** (**7**) 20 seconds. Stop motor as necessary, and push ingredients into blades with rubber spatula. **MIX** (**7**) 10 seconds or until smooth. Pour into 2 well-greased, floured 8-inch layer pans. Bake in moderate oven (350°F.) until done, 30 to 35 minutes. Cool in pans 5 minutes then turn cakes out onto wire racks to finish cooling. Yield: 2 8-inch layers.

Pecan Cake

⅔ cup pecan halves
1 package (about 17 or 18 ounces) white cake mix

Pour nuts into container. Set speed at **STIR** (**2**), then switch motor on and off as needed until nuts are coarsely chopped (see page 100). Prepare white cake mix as directed for Cake Mixes (above). Fold nuts into cake batter. Pour into 2 well-greased, floured 8-inch layer pans. Bake in moderate oven (350°F.) until done, 30 to 35 minutes. Cool layers 5 minutes before removing from pans. Finish cooling on wire rack. Yield: 2 8-inch layers.

Cakes & Frostings

Banana Layer Cake

2 cups sifted flour
2½ teaspoons baking powder
½ teaspoon salt
2 eggs
¼ cup milk
2 teaspoons vanilla
¾ cup soft shortening
1¼ cups (packed) brown sugar, broken-up
2 medium, ripe, bananas, cut in 1-inch pieces

Combine first 3 ingredients and sift into mixing bowl. **STIR** (**2**) eggs, milk, vanilla, shortening and brown sugar in container until smooth, about 40 seconds. Stop motor and push ingredients into blades with rubber spatula, as needed. Add banana pieces, pushing pieces down into mixture. **STIR** (**2**) until smooth, about 20 seconds. Turn into dry ingredients and stir just until dry ingredients are moistened. Pour into 2 well-greased, floured 8-inch layer pans. Bake in moderate oven (350°F.) until done, about 30 minutes. Yield: 2 8-inch layers.

BANANA WHIPPED CREAM CAKE—See photo at right (A). Arrange one layer of Banana Layer Cake (above) top-side-down on serving plate. Spread with Whipped Cream Cake Topping (page 36) and press thin slices of banana into topping. Cover with second cake layer, top-side-up, and spread top and sides of cake with remaining Whipped Cream Cake Topping. Serve plain or garnish with banana slices and maraschino cherry slices. Serve at once. Yield: one 2 layer cake.

BANANA BUTTERSCOTCH CAKE—Frost Banana Layer Cake (above) layers with Quick Butterscotch Frosting (page 36). Decorate top with chocolate curls or sprinkles.

A Banana Whipped Cream Cake (page 32)
with Whipped Cream Cake Topping (page 36)

B Quick Red Devil's Food Cake (page 34)
with Creamy Chocolate Frosting (page 36)

Peachy Nut Cake

1 package (about 17 to 18 ounces) yellow cake mix
¼ cup butter or margarine, melted
⅔ cup (packed) brown sugar, broken-up
½ cup pecan or walnut halves
3 tablespoons cream or milk
½ teaspoon vanilla
1 can (1 pound 13 ounces) cling peach slices, well-drained

Prepare yellow cake mix as directed for Cake Mixes (page 32). Pour into well-greased, floured 13 x 9 x 2 inch baking pan. Bake in moderate oven (350°F.) until done, 25 to 30 minutes. While cake is baking combine butter or margarine, brown sugar, nuts, cream and vanilla in container. **STIR** (**2**) until nuts are finely chopped, about 10 seconds. Spread over cake as soon as it comes from the oven and top with rows of peach slices. Broil about 5 inches from heat source until topping is bubbly and lightly browned around edges. Serve warm or cold, plain or topped with whipped cream or ice cream. Yield: One 13 x 9 x 1¾ inch cake.

Quick Red Devils Food Cake

See photo page 33 (B)

2 squares unsweetened chocolate
½ cup shortening
1 cup boiling water
2 cups sugar
½ cup buttermilk or sour milk
¼ teaspoon red food color
2 cups sifted flour
1½ teaspoons soda
½ teaspoon salt
2 eggs

Cut chocolate into small pieces and place in container. **WHIP** (**5**) turning switch on and off until finely grated. Melt shortening in boiling water and add to container. **WHIP** (**5**) at once until chocolate is melted, about 10 seconds. Add sugar; **WHIP** (**5**) 10 seconds. Add milk, food color and sifted dry ingredients. Stir with rubber spatula. **BLEND** (**10**) just until smooth, about 40 seconds. Stop motor and push ingredients into blades with rubber spatula, if necessary. Add eggs; **BLEND** (**10**) until smooth, about 10 seconds. Pour into 2 well-greased floured 8-inch layer pans. Bake in moderate oven (350°F.) until done, 30 to 35 minutes. Cool on rack 10 minutes before removing from pans. Finish cooling on rack. Frost with Creamy Chocolate Frosting (page 36). Yield: one 2 layer 8-inch cake.

Ginger Gems

2 cups sifted flour
1 teaspoon soda
1 teaspoon cinnamon
1 teaspoon ginger
2 eggs
⅔ cup molasses
½ cup soft shortening
½ cup sugar
1 cup buttermilk

Combine first 4 ingredients; sift into mixing bowl. Add eggs, molasses, shortening and sugar to container. **GRIND** (**9**) until smooth, about 25 seconds. Turn into sifted dry ingredients and add buttermilk. Stir just until dry ingredients are moistened. Fill paper cup-lined or well-greased muffin pans ⅔ full. Bake in moderate oven (375°F.) until done, about 20 minutes. Serve plain or frost with Orange Frosting (page 36). Yield: 18 to 20 cupcakes.

Sour Cream Walnut Cake

1¼ cups sifted flour
1½ teaspoons baking powder
½ teaspoon soda
½ teaspoon salt
½ cup pecan or walnut halves
2 eggs
1 cup sugar
⅓ cup cooking oil or melted shortening
2 teaspoons vanilla
½ cup dairy sour cream

Combine flour, baking powder, soda and salt and sift into mixing bowl. Set speed at **STIR** (2) then add nuts to container. Chop nuts by switching motor on and off until coarsely chopped; stir into dry ingredients. Combine remaining ingredients in container; **WHIP** (**5**) 10 seconds. Stop motor and push ingredients into blades with rubber spatula. **WHIP** (**5**) 15 to 20 seconds, or until smooth. Stop motor and push ingredients into blades with rubber spatula, as needed. Pour into 2 well-greased, floured 8-inch layer pans. Bake in moderate oven (375°F.) until done, 20 to 25 minutes. Yield: 2 8-inch layers.

Graham Cracker Cake

1¼ cups sifted flour
2 teaspoons baking powder
½ teaspoon salt
1 cup graham cracker crumbs (page 8)
1 cup milk
2 eggs
½ cup soft shortening
1 cup sugar
2 teaspoons vanilla

Sift first 3 ingredients into a bowl; stir in graham cracker crumbs. **GRIND** (9) milk, eggs, shortening, sugar and vanilla 20 seconds, or until smooth. Stop motor and push ingredients into blades with rubber spatula, as needed. Add to dry ingredients and stir just until dry ingredients are moistened. Spread into 2 well-greased, floured 8-inch layer pans. Bake in moderate oven (350°F.) until done, 18 to 20 minutes. Cool 5 minutes before removing from pans. Finish cooling on wire rack. Yield: 2 8-inch layers.

Spicy Apple Cake

2 cups sifted flour
3 teaspoons baking powder
1 teaspoon cinnamon
½ teaspoon nutmeg
½ teaspoon salt
¼ teaspoon soda
1 cup pecan or walnut halves
½ cup orange juice
½ cup soft shortening
2 eggs
1½ cups (packed) brown sugar, broken-up
1 cup seedless raisins
1 cup raw, unpeeled apple slices

Combine first 6 ingredients and sift into mixing bowl. Add nuts to container; set speed at **STIR** (**2**), then switch motor on and off until nuts are coarsely chopped. Stir into dry ingredients. Combine orange juice, shortening, eggs and sugar. **WHIP** (**5**) until smooth. Stop motor and push ingredients into blades with rubber spatula as needed. Add raisins and apples; **MIX** (**7**) until apples are finely chopped, about 10 seconds. Stop motor and push ingredients into blades with rubber spatula, as necessary. Pour into a well-greased, floured 13 x 9 x 2 inch baking pan. Bake in moderate oven (350°F.) until done, 25 to 30 minutes. Yield: One 13 x 9 x 1¼ inch cake.

Three Orange Cakes That Please

Frost **Orange Cake** (page 32) layers with **Creamy Chocolate, Orange** or **Butter Cream Frosting** (page 36). For a party cake decorate top with jelly candy orange slices or wedges or chocolate curls on the lighter frostings, or decorate edge of plate with a ring of artificial orange blossoms.

Four Fine Devils Food Cakes

Frost Quick Red Devils Food Cake (page 34) using ½ recipe of **Creamy Chocolate, Chocolate Mint, Mocha or Quick Butterscotch Frosting** (page 36).

Two Easy Pecan Cakes

Frost Pecan Cake (page 32) layers with Creamy Chocolate or Mocha Frosting (page 36).

Cream Cheese Frosting

3 tablespoons milk or cream
1 package (3 ounce) room temperature cream cheese, cubed
3 tablespoons soft butter or margarine
2 teaspoons vanilla
½ teaspoon salt
4 cups confectioners' sugar

STIR (**2**) first 5 ingredients 10 seconds or until smooth. **GRIND** (**9**) adding confectioners' sugar ¼ cup at a time. Stop motor and push ingredients into blades with rubber spatula, as needed. If frosting is very stiff and labors motor, or a stiffer frosting is desired, turn mixture into bowl and stir last bit of sugar in by hand. Yield: About 1⅔ cups.

Creamy Chocolate Frosting

See photo page 33(B)

2 packages (6 ounces each) chocolate bits
½ cup milk
3 cups confectioners' sugar
¼ cup butter or margarine
1 teaspoon salt
2 teaspoons vanilla

Place chocolate bits in container. Heat milk, 1 cup sugar, butter or margarine and salt to simmering stage. Pour into container and **GRIND** (**9**) until smooth, about 10 seconds. Add remaining sugar and vanilla, **GRIND** (**9**) until well mixed and smooth, about 20 seconds. Stop motor; push ingredients into blades with rubber spatula, as needed. Yield: About 2 cups frosting; enough to frost tops and sides of 2 8-inch layers. Use ½ recipe to top a 13 x 9 x 2 inch cake.

Quick Butterscotch Frosting

2 packages (6 ounces each) butterscotch bits
¼ cup milk
2 cups confectioners' sugar
2 tablespoons butter or margarine
½ teaspoon salt
1 teaspoon maple flavoring or vanilla

Empty bits into container. Heat milk, ¾ cup confectioners' sugar, butter or margarine and salt to simmering stage. Pour into container. **GRIND** (**9**) until smooth, about 10 seconds. Add maple flavoring or vanilla. **GRIND** (**9**) remaining confectioners' sugar, ¼ cup at a time, until smooth, after each addition, about 20 seconds. Stop motor; push ingredients into blades, as needed. Yield: About 1⅔ cups, enough to frost tops and sides of 2 8-inch layers.

CHOCOLATE MINT FROSTING—Prepare Creamy Chocolate Frosting (above); substitute **½ teaspoon mint** or **peppermint extract** for vanilla.

CHOCOLATE RUM FROSTING—Prepare Creamy Chocolate Frosting (above); substitute **½ to 1 teaspoon rum flavoring** (or to taste) for vanilla.

MOCHA FROSTING—Prepare Creamy Chocolate Frosting (above); reduce vanilla to 1 teaspoon and add **½ teaspoon instant coffee.**

Whipped Cream Cake Topping

See photo page 33(A)

½ teaspoon unflavored gelatin
2 tablespoons cold water
1 cup well-chilled whipping cream
¼ cup confectioners' sugar
½-inch square of lemon peel (yellow rind with white trimmed off)
1 teaspoon lemon juice

Stir gelatin into cold water; add 2 tablespoons cream and mix well. Place over boiling water and stir until gelatin dissolves. Pour gelatin mixture into container; add sugar, lemon peel and juice and **LIQUEFY** (**11**) just until lemon is finely chopped. Pour into bowl and chill until mixture looks like unbeaten egg whites. Whip remaining cream by turning speed to **LO** (**1**); start motor and add cream to container through top opening. Take cover off and process cream just until it thickens. Watch cream carefully—it whips quickly; fold cream into gelatin mixture. Spread on cake. Yield: Enough to top 2 8-inch cake layers. Prepare 2 separate batches of Whipped Cream Cake Topping if a generous filling and entire covering of cake is desired.

Butter Cream Frosting

⅓ cup soft butter or margarine
3 tablespoons cream or milk
2 teaspoons vanilla
⅛ teaspoon salt
3 cups confectioners' sugar

STIR (**2**) first 4 ingredients 15 seconds or until smooth. **GRIND** (**9**) adding confectioners' sugar ¼ cup at a time. Stop motor and push ingredients into blades with rubber spatula, as needed. If frosting becomes very stiff and motor labors, or a stiffer frosting is desired, turn mixture into bowl and stir last bit of confectioners' sugar in by hand. Yield: About 1⅓ cups, enough for a 13 x 9 x 2 inch cake.

ORANGE FROSTING—Prepare Butter Cream Frosting (above); omit vanilla and add **3 1-inch orange rind squares,** cut into quarters, with butter or margarine; **STIR** (**2**) until rind is very finely chopped. Substitute **orange juice** for cream or milk.

Cookies

Apricot Raisin Bars

Filling

½ cup pecan halves
1 cup dried apricots
1 cup water
1 thin slice unpeeled lemon, quartered
½ cup (packed) brown sugar, broken-up
1 tablespoon cornstarch
1 cup seedless raisins

Crust

1½ cups sifted flour
½ teaspoon baking powder
½ teaspoon salt
1 cup (packed) brown sugar, broken-up
¾ cup butter or margarine
1½ cups uncooked rolled oats, quick or regular
1 egg, beaten
1 teaspoon vanilla

FILLING: **PUREE** (**4**) pecans (see page 100) 3 to 4 seconds or until coarsely chopped; turn into saucepan. **PUREE** (**4**) apricots, water, lemon, brown sugar and cornstarch 15 seconds. Add raisins; **PUREE** (**4**) 15 seconds. Stop motor and push ingredients into blades with rubber spatula, as needed. Pour into saucepan. Cook, stirring constantly, until filling thickens. Cool.

CRUST: Sift flour, baking powder and salt into mixing bowl. Stir in brown sugar. Cut in butter or margarine with pastry blender until mixture is crumbly; stir in rolled oats. Save 2 cups of mixture for top. Add egg and vanilla to remaining mixture; mix. Spread over bottom of greased baking pan (13 x 9 x 2-inch). Spread with cooled apricot filling. Press reserved crumb mixture evenly over top. Bake in moderate oven (350°F.) until done, about 30 minutes. Cool. Cut into bars. Yield: About 36 (1 x 3-inch) bars.

Cherry Date Bars

See photo page 39 (A)

Prepare crust as directed for Apricot Raisin Bars (see recipe at left). Substitute the following Cherry Date for Apricot Raisin Filling.

Cherry Date Filling

2 thin slices unpeeled orange, quartered
1 cup water
⅓ cup sugar
2 tablespoons cornstarch
⅛ teaspoon salt
2 cups pitted dates
12 maraschino cherries

PUREE (**4**) first 5 ingredients and ½ of dates about 20 seconds. Stop motor; push ingredients into blades with rubber spatula as needed. Add remaining dates. **PUREE** (**4**) about 20 seconds, or until finely chopped. Pour into saucepan. **PUREE** (**4**) cherries 2 to 3 seconds or until coarsely chopped. Add to date mixture. Cook, stirring constantly, until thickened. Cool. Yield: Filling for 1 recipe Cherry Date Bars.

Molasses Crisps

2½ cups sifted flour
2½ teaspoons soda
¾ teaspoon cloves
1½ teaspoons cinnamon
1½ teaspoons ginger
¼ teaspoon salt
1 egg
⅓ cup molasses
1¼ cups (packed) brown sugar, broken-up
1 cup soft shortening
Granulated sugar
Cold water

Sift flour, soda, spices and salt into mixing bowl. **GRATE** (**6**) in blender; egg, molasses, brown sugar 40 to 50 seconds or until well mixed. Add shortening. **GRATE** (**6**) until smooth, about 60 seconds. Stop motor and push ingredients into blades with rubber spatula, as necessary. Turn into dry ingredients; mix well. Chill 1 to 2 hours. Roll level tablespoonfuls of dough into balls. Dip tops into sugar; place sugar side up on greased baking sheet. Sprinkle tops with 2 or 3 drops of water. Bake in moderate oven (375°F.) until done, 10 to 12 minutes. Yield: About 4 dozen cookies.

Chocolate Pecan Drops

1 cup sifted flour
1 teaspoon baking powder
½ teaspoon salt
2 eggs
½ cup soft butter or margarine
3 envelopes (1 ounce each) liquid no-melt unsweetened chocolate or 3 squares melted unsweetened chocolate
1½ teaspoons vanilla
1 cup sugar
⅔ cup pecan halves

Sift flour, baking powder and salt into mixing bowl. **STIR** (**2**) next 5 ingredients in blender until smooth, about 40 seconds. Stop motor and push ingredients into blades with rubber spatula, as necessary. Add pecans; **STIR** (**2**) 3 to 5 seconds or until nuts are coarsely chopped. Turn into dry ingredients; mix well. Chill dough several hours or overnight. Drop level tablespoonfuls of dough onto well-greased baking sheet. Bake in slow oven (325°F.) until done, 12 to 15 minutes. Yield: About 3 dozen cookies.

Date Nut Drops

2¼ cups sifted flour
1 teaspoon baking powder
½ teaspoon salt
½ teaspoon nutmeg
½ cup pecan halves
¾ cup soft butter or margarine
½ cup granulated sugar
2 eggs
1 teaspoon vanilla
1 cup (packed) brown sugar, broken-up
1 cup pitted dates
½ cup red candied cherries

Sift flour, baking powder, salt and nutmeg into mixing bowl. **GRATE** (**6**) pecans in container until coarsely chopped, 2 to 3 seconds; stir into dry ingredients. **CRUMB** (**3**) butter or margarine, granulated sugar, eggs and vanilla 30 seconds or until mixed. Stop motor; push ingredients into blades with rubber spatula as necessary. Add brown sugar; **CRUMB** (**3**) 60 seconds or until smooth and creamy. Add dates; **CRUMB** (**3**) 45 seconds or until dates are coarsely chopped. Stop motor; push ingredients into blades with rubber spatula as necessary. Add cherries; **CRUMB** (**3**) 15 seconds or until cherries are coarsely chopped. Pour over dry ingredients; mix well. Chill dough 1 hour. Drop level tablespoonfuls of dough onto greased baking sheet. Bake in moderate oven (350°F.) until done, 10 to 12 minutes. Yield: About 5½ dozen cookies.

Pineapple Oat Cookies

1½ cups sifted flour
½ teaspoon soda
½ teaspoon salt
½ teaspoon ginger
1 cup uncooked rolled oats, quick or regular
½ cup pecan halves
½ cup soft butter or margarine
1 egg
1 teaspoon vanilla
1 cup (packed) brown sugar, broken-up
1 can (8½ ounces) crushed pineapple, undrained

Sift flour, soda, salt and ginger into mixing bowl; stir in oats. **GRATE (6)** pecans in blender 2 to 3 seconds, or until coarsely chopped. Mix into dry ingredients. **CRUMB (3)** butter or margarine, egg, vanilla and ½ of the brown sugar 30 seconds or until partially mixed. Stop motor and push ingredients into blades with rubber spatula as needed. Add remaining brown sugar; **CRUMB (3)** 20 seconds or until smooth and creamy. Stop motor and push ingredients into blades with rubber spatula as needed. Add pineapple; **CRUMB (3)** 15 seconds or until mixed. Pour into dry ingredients; mix well. Chill 1 hour. Drop level tablespoonfuls of dough onto greased baking sheet. Bake in moderate oven (375°F.) until lightly browned, about 12 minutes. Yield: About 5 dozen cookies.

Almond Balls or Crescents

See photo below (C)

1½ cups sifted flour
1 cup sifted confectioners' sugar
¾ teaspoon salt
1½ cups whole blanched almonds
1 egg
1½ teaspoons vanilla
½ teaspoon almond extract
¾ cup soft butter or margarine
Confectioners' sugar

Sift flour, ½ cup confectioners' sugar and salt into mixing bowl. **PUREE (4)** almonds, ½ cup at a time in container, 10 seconds, or until nuts are very fine. Add to dry ingredients. **PUREE (4)** egg, vanilla, almond extract and remaining ½ cup confectioners' sugar 10 seconds, or until smooth. Add butter or margarine ¼ cup at a time and **PUREE (4)** 10 seconds after each addition. Stop motor and push ingredients into blades with rubber spatula, as necessary. Repeat process until smooth. Add creamed mixture to dry ingredients; mix well. Chill. Shape rounded tablespoonfuls of dough into small balls or crescents. Bake on ungreased baking sheet in moderate oven (350°F.) until done, 10 to 15 minutes. Sprinkle with confectioners' sugar while warm. Yield: About 5 dozen cookies.

MULTI-COLORED ALMOND BALLS (*See photo below* (D) — Roll unbaked Almond Balls in **red, yellow, green** or **pink sugars.** Bake as directed for Almond Balls.

C
F
I
A
C
B

GLAZED ALMOND COOKIES (See photo page 38) (E)—Prepare Almond Balls or Crescent dough. Shape dough into 3 smooth rolls, 6 inches long. Wrap and chill. Before baking roll each cookie roll in **colored or granulated sugar.** Cut into slices ¼ inch thick. Bake on ungreased baking sheet, in moderate oven (350°F.) until done, about 10 minutes. Spread tops with favorite **thick preserves or confectioners' sugar frosting.** Cool. Yield: About 6 dozen cookies.

Date Nut Bars

See photo page 39 (F)

1 cup sifted flour
1 teaspoon baking powder
½ teaspoon salt
1½ cups pecan or walnut halves
3 eggs
1 cup sugar
1 teaspoon vanilla
1½ cups pitted dates
Confectioners' sugar, optional

Sift flour, baking powder and salt into bowl. **PUREE (4)** nuts (see page 100), one half cup at a time, about 3 to 4 seconds or until coarsely chopped; turn into dry ingredients. **PUREE (4)** eggs, sugar and vanilla 10 seconds. Add dates; **PUREE (4)** about 20 seconds or until dates are coarsely chopped. Pour over dry ingredients; mix well. Spread into greased baking pan (13 x 9 x 2 inches). Bake in slow oven (325°F.) until done, about 30 minutes. Cool. Cut into bars; serve plain or dust with confectioners' sugar. Yield: About 36 bars 1 x 3 inches.

FRUIT ALMOND BARS *See photo page 38 (G)*—Follow recipe for Date Nut Bars; substitute **1 cup whole blanched almonds** for pecans or walnuts, **1 cup mixed chopped candied fruits** and **½ cup red candied cherries** for the dates. **PUREE (4)** cherries with egg mixture 3 to 4 seconds or until coarsely chopped and proceed as for Date Nut Bars.

Chocolate Pecan Brownies

See photo page 38 (H)

¾ cup sifted flour
½ teaspoon baking powder
½ teaspoon salt
2 eggs
3 envelopes (1 ounce each) liquid no-melt unsweetened chocolate or 3 squares unsweetened chocolate, melted
⅓ cup soft butter or margarine
1 cup sugar
1 teaspoon vanilla
1 cup pecan halves

Sift flour, baking powder and salt into bowl. **PUREE (4)** next 5 ingredients in blender 30 seconds, or until smooth. Add pecans; **PUREE (4)** 10 seconds, or until pecans are coarsely chopped. Pour over dry ingredients; mix well. Turn into greased 8-inch square pan. Bake in moderate oven (350°F.) until done, about 30 minutes. Cool on rack. Frost with Creamy Chocolate Frosting (page 36), if desired. Yield: 16 2-inch squares.

Rum Balls

1½ cups pecan halves
1¾ cups very fine blender-made cookie crumbs (page 8)
1 cup sifted confectioners' sugar
1 tablespoon cocoa
⅛ teaspoon salt
⅓ cup light corn syrup
3 tablespoons rum
1 teaspoon vanilla
Sifted confectioners' sugar for rolling balls

GRATE (6) pecans (see page 100) 4 to 5 seconds or until finely chopped. Turn into mixing bowl. Add crumbs, sugar, cocoa and salt; mix well with pastry blender. Add syrup, rum and vanilla; mix well and shape into compact balls using 1 tablespoonful of mixture for each ball. Roll balls in confectioners' sugar. Allow to dry several hours. Store in air-tight container to mellow. Yield: About 2 dozen balls.

BRANDY BALLS — Follow recipe for Rum Balls and substitute **brandy** for rum.

CRÈME DE MENTHE BALLS — Follow recipe for Rum Balls and substitute **crème de menthe** for rum and roll balls in **chocolate sprinkles** rather than confectioners' sugar.

Banana Oat Munchies

1½ cups sifted flour
1½ teaspoons baking powder
1 teaspoon salt
½ teaspoon cinnamon
¼ teaspoon nutmeg
1½ cups uncooked rolled oats, quick or regular
1 egg
¾ cup soft shortening
1 cup sugar
1 teaspoon vanilla
2 medium bananas, sliced
¾ cup pecan halves

Sift first 5 ingredients into mixing bowl. Stir in rolled oats. **STIR** (**2**) in container; egg, shortening, sugar and vanilla until smooth, about 60 seconds. Stop motor and push ingredients into blades with rubber spatula as needed. Add ½ of banana slices, **STIR** (**2**) until bananas are well mashed, about 20 seconds. Stop motor and push ingredients into blades as needed. Add remaining bananas; **STIR** (**2**) until well mashed, about 20 seconds. Add pecans; **STIR** (**2**) 15 seconds or until nuts are coarsely chopped. Turn into dry ingredients; mix well. Chill. Drop level tablespoonfuls of dough onto well-greased baking sheet. Bake in moderate oven (375°F.) until done, about 15 minutes. Yield: About 5 dozen cookies.

Banana Nut Cookies

2¼ cups sifted flour
2 teaspoons baking powder
¼ teaspoon baking soda
¾ teaspoon salt
½ cup nuts
2 eggs
⅔ cup soft shortening
1 cup sugar
1 teaspoon vanilla
2 medium bananas, cut in 1-inch pieces

Sift first 4 ingredients into mixing bowl. **PUREE** (**4**) nuts in blender (see page 100), until coarsely chopped, 3 to 4 seconds. Stir into flour mixture. **PUREE** (**4**) eggs, shortening, sugar and vanilla 45 seconds or until smooth. Stop motor and push ingredients into blades with rubber spatula as needed. Add bananas. **PUREE** (**4**) 30 seconds or until smooth. Pour into dry ingredients; stir until well blended. Drop level tablespoonfuls of dough onto lightly greased baking sheet. Bake in moderate oven (375°F.) 8 to 10 minutes or until done and lightly browned. Yield: About 5½ dozen cookies.

Peanut Drop Cookies

See photo page 38 (B&I)

3 cups sifted flour
2 teaspoons baking powder
2 eggs
⅓ cup milk
1 teaspoon vanilla
¾ cup soft butter or margarine
1 cup sugar
1 cup salted peanuts

Sift flour and baking powder into mixing bowl. **STIR** (**2**) next 5 ingredients in container until well mixed, about 60 seconds. Stop motor and push ingredients into blades with rubber spatula, as needed. Add peanuts. **STIR** (**2**) until peanuts are coarsely chopped, about 10 seconds. Stop motor and push ingredients into blades with rubber spatula, as needed. Add to dry ingredients; mix well. Chill well. Drop tablespoonfuls of dough onto well-greased baking sheet. Bake in moderate oven (350°F.) until done and lightly browned, 12 to 15 minutes. Spread with favorite chocolate or butterscotch frosting (page 36) garnish with chopped nut or pecan halves. Yield: About 5 dozen cookies.

Apple Raisin Drops

2 cups sifted flour
1 teaspoon baking powder
1 teaspoon cinnamon
½ teaspoon nutmeg
½ teaspoon salt
½ cup seedless raisins
½ cup pecan halves
2 eggs
½ cup soft butter or margarine
1 cup (packed) brown sugar, broken-up
2 cups coarsely chopped unpeeled apple

Sift flour, baking powder, spices and salt into mixing bowl. Stir in raisins. Place pecans in container; set speed at **GRATE** (**6**) then switch motor on and off until nuts are coarsely chopped. Add to dry ingredients. **CRUMB** (**3**) eggs, butter or margarine and ½ of the brown sugar 30 seconds or until well mixed. Add remaining brown sugar; **CRUMB** (**3**) 30 seconds or until well mixed. **CRUMB** (**3**) apple, ⅓ at a time, 15 seconds or until apple is finely chopped. Pour over dry ingredients; mix well. Chill 1 hour. Drop level tablespoonfuls of dough onto greased baking sheet. Bake in moderate oven (375°F.) until lightly browned, 12 to 15 minutes. Yield: About 5 dozen cookies.

Frozen Nesselrode Pudding

See photo at right

½ cup whole blanched almonds
⅓ cup red maraschino cherries, halved
⅓ cup green maraschino cherries, halved
2 packages (3 ounces each) vanilla pudding and pie filling (not instant)
½ cup sugar
4 cups milk
1½ teaspoons ground mace or nutmeg
½ cup chopped, mixed candied fruit
¼ cup vanilla wafer or macaroon crumbs
2 tablespoons rum or 2 teaspoons rum extract
2 teaspoons vanilla
4 cups whipped cream or dessert topping

Add almonds to container; set speed at **STIR** (**2**) then switch motor on and off quickly, until nuts are chopped medium fine (see page 100). Turn into bowl. Coarsely chop red and green cherries in same manner as nuts leaving pieces rather large. Prepare pudding with sugar and milk as directed on package label. Stir in mace or nutmeg, cherries and candied fruits. Chill, stirring often. Stir in almonds, crumbs and flavorings; fold in whipped cream or dessert topping. Spoon into fancy 2 quart mold or 9 x 5 x 3 inch loaf pan. Freeze. To unmold dip mold in warm water quickly, dry outside of mold and turn onto chilled serving dish. Return to freezer to harden. Serve plain or garnish with additional whipped cream or dessert topping and maraschino cherry slices, if desired. Yield: About 12 servings.

Strawberry Mousse

¼ cup milk
¼ cup sugar
4 cups (about 7 ounces) miniature marshmallows
1 package (1 pound) frozen strawberries, partially defrosted, cubed
1 teaspoon vanilla
2 cups whipped cream or dessert topping

Heat milk and sugar to scalding stage. Empty marshmallows into container; add hot milk and **CRUMB** (**3**) until smooth, about 25 seconds. Add strawberries and vanilla, **CRUMB** (**3**) until well mixed, about 15 seconds. Pour into bowl, and fold in whipped cream or dessert topping. Pour into 9 x 5 x 3 inch loaf pan. Freeze. Serve plain or with strawberry or chocolate sauce. Yield: About 5 cups.

Desserts

Chilled Orange Soufflés

See photo at right

1 can (1 pound) apricot halves
¾ cup sugar
½ teaspoon salt
4 eggs, separated
2 envelopes (1-tablespoon each) unflavored gelatin
¼-inch slice unpeeled orange, quartered
2 cups whipped cream or dessert topping

Wrap heavy waxed paper collars (2 or 3 papers thick and 2 inches wide) tightly around edge of 8 small individual soufflé dishes, demitasse or custard cups; fasten securely. Saving 1 cup syrup, drain apricots. Combine ½ cup sugar, salt, the reserved 1 cup syrup, egg yolks and gelatin in container. **STIR** (**2**) until well mixed, about 5 seconds. Pour into saucepan; cook over very low heat, stirring constantly, until mixture will coat a metal spoon. Combine apricots and orange slice in container; **BLEND** (**10**) until fruit is very finely chopped, about 20 seconds. Stir fruit into custard mixture. Chill until mixture starts to thicken. Beat egg whites, with electric or hand beater, until they hold soft peaks and add remaining ¼ cup sugar gradually. Continue beating until egg whites are stiff and glossy. Fold gelatin mixture and whipped cream or dessert topping into egg whites. Spoon into collared dishes. Chill until firm. Remove waxed paper collars and serve. If desired, garnish each dessert with small orange sections and mint sprigs. Yield: 8 servings.

Viennese Angel Dessert

Slice a round bakery **angel food cake** into 4 even layers. Spread each layer with **Peachy Apricot Jam** (page 72). Reassemble layers. Spread top and sides of cake with **Creamy Chocolate Frosting** (page 36). Chill. Yield: 8 to 12 servings.

Frozen Nesselrode Pudding

Chilled Orange Soufflé

Chocolate Parfait

See photo at right

1 pint vanilla ice cream
Fudge Sauce (page 85)
Whipped cream or dessert topping

Spoon alternate layers of ice cream and Fudge Sauce into chilled parfait or dessert glasses. Top with whipped cream or dessert topping. Yield: About 4 servings.

STRAWBERRY PARFAIT—Follow recipe for Chocolate Parfait and substitute **Quick Strawberry Sundae Sauce** (page 85) for Fudge Sauce. Yield: About 4 servings.

Custard

2 eggs or 4 egg yolks
2 cups milk
⅓ cup sugar
1½ teaspoons vanilla
¼ teaspoon salt
¼ teaspoon nutmeg

Combine ingredients in container. Set speed at **STIR** (**2**); then turn switch on and off 3 or 4 times to mix. Pour into 4 or 5 buttered 5 ounce custard cups. Set cups in pan of shallow hot water. Bake in moderate oven (350°F.) 25 to 30 minutes or until knife inserted in center comes out clean. Chill. Unmold; serve plain or topped with defrosted frozen or fresh fruit, Fudge or Butterscotch Dessert Sauce (page 85), if desired. Yield: 4 to 5 servings.

COFFEE CUSTARD—Follow recipe for Custard, above. Substitute **1½ teaspoons of instant coffee** for nutmeg.

MAPLE CUSTARD—Follow **Custard** recipe (above). Substitute **brown** for granulated **sugar.** Omit nutmeg and vanilla and add **½ teaspoon maple flavoring.**

CRÈME BRÛLÉE—Follow **Custard** recipe (above) and substitute **whipping cream or half and half** (**half milk half cream**) for milk, increase eggs to 3 and omit nutmeg. Bake in buttered individual soufflé dishes or custard cups. Chill until serving time then top each custard with **2 teaspoons brown sugar** and pack dishes in crushed ice. Broil 4 inches from heat just until sugar melts and caramelizes. Serve at once. Yield: 4 to 5 servings.

Chocolate Parfait

Quick Fruit Ice

½ of 6 ounce can frozen orange, tangerine, boysenberry, pineapple or grape juice concentrate, partially defrosted
2 cups crushed ice

Combine ingredients in container; **BLEND (10)** just until smooth and consistency of commercial ice or sherbet, about 40 seconds. Stop motor and quickly push ingredients into blades once during processing, if needed. Serve at once with straws or spoon. Yield: About 1 pint, 2 to 3 servings.

Flaming Fruit Dessert

1 can (1 pound 4 ounces) whole blue plums
1 can (1 pound) peach halves
¼ inch slice unpeeled lemon, quartered
½ cup sugar
12 whole cloves
2 sticks cinnamon
2 tablespoons brandy, optional

Saving syrups, drain fruit. Remove seeds from ½ of plums; place in container with 1 cup of the reserved fruit syrup and add lemon and sugar. **STIR (2)** until plums are very finely chopped, 3 to 5 seconds. Stop motor and push ingredients into blades if needed. Turn into saucepan; add spices and remaining reserved fruit syrup. Bring sauce to a boil; simmer 2 to 3 minutes. Pour over remaining fruit; refrigerate 2 to 3 hours. At serving time heat in chafing dish. Pour slightly heated brandy over sauce; ignite and serve when flame dies down. If preferred, omit brandy and serve chilled with cake or cookies. Yield: About 4 cups or 8 servings.

Dessert Pancakes

See photo below

Thin Pancakes (page 30)
½ cup dairy sour cream
1 package (8 ounces) room temperature cream cheese, cubed
2 tablespoons sugar
1 cup orange marmalade
¼ cup orange juice
2 tablespoons butter or margarine
¼ cup orange flavored liqueur, optional

Prepare pancakes; keep warm. Combine sour cream, ½ of cheese and sugar in container. **STIR (2)** until smooth, about 6 seconds. Add remaining cheese; **STIR (2)** until smooth. Stop motor and push ingredients into blades, as needed. Spread an equal amount of cheese mixture over each pancake; roll up. Combine marmalade and orange juice; heat. Heat pancakes in skillet in butter or margarine; top with orange marmalade mixture. If desired, ladle slightly heated orange liqueur over pancakes; ignite and serve when flame dies down. Yield: 12 pancakes.

Dessert Pancakes

Peach Crisp

1 cup pecan halves
¾ cup blender-chopped graham cracker crumbs (page 8)
½ cup (packed) brown sugar, broken-up
½ teaspoon cinnamon
½ teaspoon nutmeg
¼ teaspoon salt
⅓ cup melted butter or margarine
1 can (1 pound 13 ounce) sliced peaches
Whipped cream or dessert topping, optional

Chop pecans in container, ½ cup at a time. Set speed at **STIR** (**2**) then switch motor on and off until nuts are coarsely chopped (see page 100). Pour into bowl and add crumbs. Combine sugar, spices and salt in container. **STIR** (**2**) until mixed 2 to 4 seconds. Pour into bowl. Add butter or margarine; mix well. Drain peaches; save ½ cup syrup. Spread peaches over bottom of lightly buttered shallow baking dish (11 x 7 x 1½ inches). Sprinkle with crumb mixture. Drizzle peach syrup over top. Bake in moderate oven (375°F.) until hot and bubbly around edges, about 25 minutes. Serve warm or cold, plain or with cream. Yield: About 4 to 6 servings.

Chocolate Pecan Ice Cream

¾ cup pecan halves
1 package (6 ounce) semi-sweet chocolate bits
4 cups (about 7 ounces) miniature marshmallows
1 cup milk
¼ cup sugar
½ teaspoon salt
1 teaspoon vanilla
2 cups whipped cream or dessert topping

Pour nuts into container. Set speed at **STIR** (**2**) then switch motor on and off as needed to coarsely chop (see page 100). Empty into bowl. Combine chocolate and marshmallows in container. Combine milk, sugar and salt in saucepan; heat to simmering stage. Pour into container and add vanilla. **GRATE** (**6**) until smooth, about 15 seconds. Pour into 9 x 5 x 3 inch loaf pan or freezer trays. Freeze until firm. Cut into small chunks; place in container. **STIR** (**2**) until smooth, about 40 seconds. Stop motor and push ingredients into blades with rubber spatula, as needed. Pour into well chilled bowl. Fold in whipped cream or dessert topping and nuts. Pour into 9 x 5 x 3 inch loaf pan. Freeze. Yield: About 4 cups.

Cheese Blintzes

12 thin pancakes (page 30)
1½ cups creamed cottage cheese
2 1-inch squares lemon rind
2 egg yolks
1 teaspoon vanilla
2 tablespoons sugar
½ teaspoon salt
¼ teaspoon cinnamon
1 package (3 ounce) room temperature cream cheese, cubed
3 tablespoons butter or margarine

Prepare thin pancakes, browning cakes well on one side only. For filling combine next 7 ingredients, in order listed, in container. **STIR** (**2**) until smooth, 20 to 30 seconds. Add cream cheese and **STIR** (**2**) until well mixed, 20 to 30 seconds. Stop motor and push ingredients into blades with rubber spatula as necessary. Spoon filling across center of browned side of each pancake. Turn edges in and roll. Cover and store in refrigerator until serving time. To heat, melt butter or margarine in frypan or chafing dish over direct high flame. Brown and heat blintzes, turning once. Serve hot with sour cream and preserves or Quick Strawberry Sundae Sauce (page 85). Yield: 12 blintzes.

Ice Cream Treats

Icy Fruit Delights

Combine in blender container 1 can (6-ounce) frozen lemonade or limeade, ½ cup corn syrup and water called for in mixing directions on can label. **BLEND (10)** until mixed, 2 to 4 seconds. Pour into cone shaped paper cups, aluminum foil corn stick pans or paddle pop molds. Freeze until partially solid. Push wooden craft-sticks or small wooden tongue depressors into center of one end so handle will stay in during eating. Freeze hard. Yield: 2½ cups, about 6 to 8 servings.

Snow Cones

See photo at right

2½ cups crushed ice
1 cup cold water
6 tablespoons syrup (fruit flavored soda, sundae or pancake syrup, defrosted frozen grape, orange, tangerine or boysenberry concentrate diluted with an equal part of water, or light colored syrup flavored with fruit, mint or maple extract and tinted with desired food color)

BLEND (10) ice and water in container just until finely crushed, 30 to 40 seconds. Empty into sieve; drain off water quickly. Pile ice into paper or plastic cups. Drizzle 3 tablespoons syrup over ice in each cup. Serve at once with straw or spoon. Yield: About 2 cups; 2 servings.

Ice Cream Treats

See photo at left

Cut pint bricks of **vanilla, strawberry** or **chocolate ice cream** into 3 even slices. Push ½ the length of a paddle (craftstick or small tongue depressor) into center of one end of each ice cream slice. Cover ice cream with **blender-chopped peanut brittle, peppermint stick candy, chopped nuts or chocolate bits** by pressing each side of ice cream slice into crumbs. Place in freezer to harden. To chop candies (page 9) break into small pieces. Put a small amount of candy, nuts or chocolate bits into container at a time. Set speed at **CRUMB (3)** then switch motor on and off quickly until chopped to desired fineness.

Charcoal Broiled Chuck Steak

See photo page 55

1 thick (about 2 inch) beef chuck steak, 4 to 5 pounds
Instant meat tenderizer
Herb or Garlic Butter (page 93), melted
Barbecue (page 84) or Steak or Burger Sauce (page 82)

Start charcoal fire 40 minutes ahead of time so coals will have a coating of gray ash and give off a uniform heat. Trim excess fat from steak so it won't drip onto coals causing flame-up. Slash remaining fat (avoid cutting into meat) around edge so steak will remain flat and broil evenly. Spread coals ½ inch apart to reduce flame-up. Sprinkle steak on both sides with meat tenderizer as directed on package label. Rub hot grill with fat. Broil steak 4 to 5 inches above a bed of coals covered with gray ash. Broil first side about 20 minutes, for medium rare, turn and broil second side an equal time. Baste steak frequently during broiling with Herb or Garlic Butter. To check steak for doneness make a small slash in center of steak with sharp pointed knife and examine color. Continue broiling if desired. Serve with Barbecue or Steak or Burger Sauce. Yield: 6 to 8 servings.

Charcoal Broiled Steak

1 large porterhouse or top quality sirloin steak, 1½ to 2 inches thick
Herb-Wine Vinegar Marinade (page 49)
Garlic Butter (page 93), melted
Bearnaise Sauce (page 83) or Steak or Burger Sauce (page 82)

Trim excess fat from steak and slash remaining fat on edge so steak will remain flat during broiling. Place steak in large shallow dish or large plastic bag on tray. Pour Herb-Wine Vinegar Marinade over steak and tie plastic bag at both ends. Refrigerate 2 to 4 hours, turning steak 3 or 4 times. Drain steak and broil on greased grill 3 to 4 inches above a bed of hot charcoal, about 20 minutes per side for medium rare steak. Brush steak frequently during broiling with Garlic Butter. To check for degree of doneness, make a small slash in center of steak with sharp pointed knife; check color of meat and continue broiling, if desired. Serve with Bearnaise or Steak or Burger Sauce. Yield: About 4 servings of porterhouse or 6 of sirloin.

Lobster Thermidor

4 frozen lobster tails (about 6 ounces each)
1 cup Rich Cream Sauce (medium) (page 81)
¼ cup cooked diced celery
2 tablespoons sherry
1 teaspoon lemon juice
¼ teaspoon dry mustard
3 tablespoons blender-grated Parmesan cheese (page 100)
3 tablespoons corn flake crumbs (page 8)
Paprika

Clean lobster tails and boil as directed on package label. Cut tails open lengthwise through outer shell. Remove meat from shell; cut into ½-inch cubes. Save shells. Combine hot Rich Cream Sauce, celery, sherry, lemon juice and mustard and mix. Fold in lobster. Spoon into lobster tail shells. Combine cheese and crumbs; sprinkle over lobster mixture. Sprinkle with paprika. Brown in moderate oven (375°F.) until hot, about 10 minutes. Yield: 4 servings.

Charcoal Broiled Lobster Tails

See photo page 55

6 frozen lobster tails (6 to 8 ounces each), defrosted
Lemon Parsley Butter (page 93)

Cut off undershells of lobster tails with scissors. Cut six 12-inch squares of heavy-duty aluminum foil. Place a lobster tail on each. Brush lobster meat with Lemon Parsley Butter. Bring foil up over the tail; fold and crimp edges together. Place packages on grill, shell side down, about 5 inches above low glowing coals. Heat 20 minutes. Remove tails from foil and place tails on grill, flesh side down, until lightly browned, 2 to 3 minutes. Serve with Lemon Parsley Butter. Yield: 6 servings.

Herb-Wine Vinegar Marinade

1 cup salad oil
1 cup red wine or cider vinegar
2 thin slices onion
2 ¼-inch slices unpeeled lemon or lime, quartered
2 cloves garlic, sliced
1 teaspoon fines herbes blend
1 teaspoon salt
⅛ teaspoon pepper

PUREE (**4**) all ingredients in container until lemon or lime peel and garlic are finely chopped, about 15 seconds. Use as marinade for steaks or roasts. Yield: About 2 cups.

Savory Barbecue Chicken

2 frying chickens (3 pounds each)
⅔ cup salad oil
⅔ cup wine or cider vinegar
⅔ cup catsup
1 clove garlic, sliced
1 teaspoon salt
¼ teaspoon pepper
Melted butter or margarine
Barbecue Sauce (page 84)

Cut chickens into serving pieces. Place in bowl or large plastic bag. Combine next 6 ingredients in container; **STIR** (**2**) until garlic is minced, 3 to 4 seconds. Pour over chicken pieces. Cover or close bag. Refrigerate 2 to 3 hours. Drain. Place pieces on grill over medium charcoal fire and brush with melted butter or margarine. Cook 40 to 50 minutes until chicken is very tender. Turn pieces often, basting with butter or margarine after each turning. Baste chicken with Barbecue Sauce during last 10 to 15 minutes, as desired. Serve with Barbecue Sauce. Yield: 8 servings.

Barbecued Chicken

Cut cleaned **frying chicken** into quarters or serving pieces. Place pieces, skin side up, on greased grill over medium charcoal fire and cook until tender, 40 to 50 minutes, turning pieces every 4 to 6 minutes. Brush with melted **Herb, Lemon Parsley or Chili Butter** (page 93) each time chicken pieces are turned. Serve plain or with **Barbecue Sauce** (page 84). Yield: Allow ¾ of a pound per person.

Charcoal Broiled Burgers

See photo page 55

2 pounds ground beef chuck, round or hamburger meat
1½ teaspoons salt
½ teaspoon onion salt
¼ teaspoon pepper
2 eggs
Garlic, Chili, Italian or Onion Butter (page 93)
Barbecue, Bearnaise, Steak or Burger Sauce (pages 82 to 84)

Combine first 5 ingredients; mix well. Shape into 8 large patties. Brush with melted Garlic, Chili, Italian or Onion Butter. Broil on greased rack about 4 inches above a bed of medium charcoal. Cook to desired doneness, 10 to 15 minutes, turning once and brushing with selected butter. Serve with Barbecue, Bearnaise, Steak or Burger Sauce desired. Yield: 8 large burgers.

OVEN-BROILED BURGERS—Prepare as directed (above) for Charcoal Broiled Burgers. Broil 3 to 4 inches from broiler heat source to desired degree of doneness, 15 to 20 minutes, turning burgers once.

Shrimp Jambalaya

1 cup ¾-inch diced ham
1 can (1 pound 12 ounces) tomatoes
1 can (8 ounces) tomato sauce
⅓ cup water
1 small clove garlic, sliced
1 small onion, sliced and quartered
1 cup 1-inch green pepper squares
¾ teaspoon salt
¼ teaspoon leaf thyme
¼ teaspoon pepper
1 cup uncooked rice, not pre-cooked
2 or 3 cans (4½ ounces each) deveined small shrimp, drained
Parsley, optional

Add ham to container. Set speed at **LO** (**1**) then switch motor on and off 2 or 3 times, or just until ham is very coarsely chopped. Empty container and add next 9 ingredients. **STIR** (**2**) just until onions and green peppers are coarsely chopped, 4 to 5 seconds. Pour into large skillet or Dutch oven; stir in rice. Cover and cook slowly until rice is tender, 25 to 30 minutes. Add ham and shrimp; mix carefully and heat to serving temperature, 8 to 10 minutes. Garnish with parsley, if desired. Yield: About 6 servings.

Sloppy Joes For a Crowd

1½ cups catsup
1 cup water
3 medium onions (2-inch), sliced and quartered
2½ tablespoons flour
1½ teaspoons salt
1¼ teaspoons chili powder
¼ teaspoon pepper
2 tablespoons shortening
1½ pounds ground beef chuck, round or hamburger meat

Combine first 7 ingredients in container. Set speed at **STIR** (**2**) then turn switch on and off 3 or 4 times or just until onions are coarsely chopped. Heat shortening in large skillet. Add meat and cook on moderate heat until gray in color, stirring as needed to gray evenly. Add tomato-onion mixture; mix well. Simmer uncovered until meat is cooked and mixture thickened, about 20 minutes. Yield: About 4 cups, enough for 12 to 16 sandwiches.

Mexican Rarebit

1 recipe Blender Rarebit (page 53)
½ teaspoon chili powder
2 dashes Tabasco Sauce
¼ cup diced (¼-inch) green pepper
1 medium tomato, washed, stemmed and diced (½-inch)

Prepare as directed for Blender Rarebit. Add ingredients to mixture just before heating. Yield: About 2¼ cups.

Sweet 'N Sour Sauce

See photos pages 55 and 82

1 can (13½ ounces) pineapple tidbits
1 clove garlic, sliced
2 thin slices unpeeled lemon, quartered
2 tablespoons cornstarch
2 tablespoons soy sauce
1 teaspoon ginger
1 jar (12 ounces) pineapple preserves

Using syrup from drained tidbits, combine with garlic, lemon, cornstarch, soy sauce and ginger in container; **GRATE** (**6**) 15 seconds, or until lemon is finely chopped. Pour into saucepan; add preserves and tidbits. Cook over low heat, stirring constantly, until thick and clear. Yield: About 2½ cups sauce.

Sweet 'N Sour Spareribs

See photo page 55

Cut **5 pounds of spareribs** in 3 to 6 rib portions. Arrange ribs on grill 5 inches above low bed of charcoal. Spread briquets ½ inch apart to avoid flame-up. Spareribs, like all cuts of pork, require long, slow cooking and must be barbecued to the well-done stage. During barbecuing, turn ribs every 2 or 3 minutes and baste at each turn with **Sweet 'N Sour Sauce** (at left). Barbecued spareribs are done when the meat pulls away from the bones. Serve with remaining sauce. Yield: 5 to 6 servings.

Cheese Squares With Vegetable or Ham Sauce

2 cups scalded milk
¼ pound American cheese, in ½-inch cubes
1 slice small onion
1 tablespoon flour
4 sprigs parsley, no stems
1½ teaspoons salt
⅛ teaspoon pepper
1 teaspoon prepared mustard
3 eggs
3 cups hot cooked rice
Creamy Vegetable or Ham Sauce (below)

Set speed at **PUREE** (**4**) and pour hot milk into container. Start motor and add cheese cubes through **top opening,** quickly, one cube at a time, processing until all cubes are added, about 45 seconds. Add next 6 ingredients. **PUREE** (**4**) 5 seconds. Add eggs, one at a time. Set speed at **LO** (**1**) and then switch motor on and off after each addition. Pour mixture over rice; mix. Pour into buttered shallow 1½ quart baking dish. Bake in slow oven (325°F.) until set, about 45 minutes. Cool 5 minutes; cut in squares and serve with Creamy Vegetable or Ham Sauce. Yield: 6 servings.

CREAMY VEGETABLE OR HAM SAUCE—Prepare ½ recipe of **Quick White Sauce, Medium** (page 81). Stir in **⅔ cup** well drained cooked **mixed vegetables** or **chopped ham** and heat. Yield: About 1½ cups sauce.

Country Captain Chicken

See photo below (A)

1 can (1 pound) tomatoes
1 clove garlic, sliced
1 medium onion, quartered
1 medium green pepper, cut in eighths
¼ cup flour
3 teaspoons curry powder
1½ teaspoons salt
½ teaspoon leaf thyme
¼ teaspoon pepper
1 frying chicken (3 pounds), cut in serving pieces
¼ cup butter or margarine
¼ cup currants or raisins
¼ cup toasted slivered almonds, optional
Hot fluffy rice

Combine tomatoes, garlic, onion and green pepper in container. Set speed at **PUREE** (**4**) and turn switch on and off several times, until vegetables are coarsely chopped. Combine in a bowl: flour, curry powder, salt, thyme and pepper. Dredge chicken pieces in flour mixture. Brown chicken in frying pan in butter or margarine, turning to brown evenly. Sprinkle with any remaining flour mixture. Add tomato mixture and currants or raisins. Cover and cook slowly until chicken is fork tender, about 45 minutes. Sprinkle chicken with almonds, if desired and serve with rice. Yield: About 6 servings.

Macaroni and Cheese

See photo below (B)

¾ cup corn flakes
1 recipe Cheese Sauce (page 81)
1 teaspoon prepared mustard
2 thin slices onion
1 package (7 ounces) elbow macaroni, cooked and drained
¾ cup cubed (½-inch) American or Cheddar cheese
¼ cup diced pimiento
2 tablespoons butter or margarine, melted

Add corn flakes to container. Set speed at **PUREE** (**4**) then switch motor on and off until flakes are coarsely chopped, about 4 times. (Should make about ⅓ cup coarse crumbs.) Empty container and save crumbs. Combine ingredients for a Cheese Sauce (medium), mustard and onion in container. **PUREE** (**4**) until onion is finely chopped, 8 to 10 seconds. Prepare as directed for Cheese Sauce. Combine sauce, macaroni, cheese cubes and pimiento; mix. Spoon into buttered 1½ quart casserole or 4 to 6 individual ramekins. Mix corn flake crumbs and butter or margarine and sprinkle around edges of casserole or ramekins. Bake in moderate oven (350°F.) until hot and bubbly about 30 minutes. Yield: 4 to 6 servings.

B

A

Tuna Burgers

1 cup catsup or chili sauce
1 cup water
3 tablespoons sugar
2 tablespoons vinegar or lemon juice
¼-inch slice unpeeled lemon, quartered
1 tablespoon Worcestershire sauce
1 teaspoon salt
½ teaspoon chili powder
2 dashes Tabasco sauce
1 medium onion, sliced and quartered
½ cup (½-inch) celery slices
⅓ cup (1-inch) green pepper squares
2 cans (7 ounces each) solid pack tuna, drained and flaked
Toasted buttered hamburger buns

Combine first 9 ingredients in container. **STIR** (**2**) until mixed, 3 to 4 seconds. Add onion, celery and green pepper. Set speed at **STIR** (**2**) then turn switch on just until vegetables at top travel to blades. Turn motor off at once. Turn into saucepan; simmer slowly to blend flavors, about 25 minutes. Add tuna; heat about 10 minutes, stirring frequently. Serve on hot toasted buns. Yield: About 4 cups, enough for 8 large sandwiches.

Wheat Germ Meat Loaf

2 pounds ground beef chuck, round or hamburger meat
¾ cup soft bread crumbs (see page 100)
½ cup wheat germ
1 can (8 ounces) tomato sauce or 1 cup catsup
1 medium onion, sliced and quartered
¼ green pepper, cut into 1-inch squares
2 eggs
2 teaspoons salt
½ teaspoon pepper

Combine first 3 ingredients in mixing bowl. Add remaining ingredients to container. Set speed at **CRUMB** (**3**) then switch motor on and off as needed to coarsely chop onion and green pepper, 6 or 7 times. Add to meat mixture; mix well. Pack into loaf pan (9 x 5 x 3 inch). Bake in moderate oven (350°F.) until done, about 60 minutes. Cool in pan 10 minutes before removing. Serve hot or cold, plain or with Cheese Sauce (page 81), if desired. Yield: 1 loaf 9 x 5 x 2½ inches, about 8 servings.

Spaghetti With Meat Sauce

2 pounds ground beef, chuck or round
3 tablespoons shortening
2 cans (8 ounces each) tomato sauce
1 can (6 ounces) tomato paste
¾ cup water
1 clove garlic, sliced
2 medium onions, quartered and sliced
1 tablespoon Worcestershire sauce
2 beef bouillon cubes
1½ teaspoons salt
½ teaspoon sugar
1 can (1 pound 12 ounces) tomatoes
8 servings hot, cooked, seasoned spaghetti
Blender-grated Parmesan cheese (page 100)

Heat meat in hot shortening in large Dutch oven, stirring often, until meat is gray in color. Add 1 can tomato sauce and the tomato paste to meat. Add remaining tomato sauce, water and next 6 ingredients to container. **CRUMB** (**3**) until onions are finely chopped. Empty sauce mixture into Dutch oven. Add tomatoes to container; set speed at **STIR** (**2**), turn switch on and off quickly 1 or 2 times, add tomatoes to sauce mixture. Cover. Simmer gently over low heat until sauce is thick and flavors are well blended, about 40 minutes. Serve on hot spaghetti and top with Parmesan cheese. Yield: 8 servings.

Deviled Crab Crêpes

1 recipe Thin Pancakes for Crêpes and Blintzes (page 30)
1½ recipes Rich Cream Sauce (Thick) (page 81)
½ teaspoon curry powder
½ teaspoon Worcestershire sauce
¼ teaspoon onion salt
Dash of Tabasco sauce
1 cup flaked crab meat
1 recipe Hollandaise Sauce (page 84)
¼ cup white wine, optional

Prepare pancakes; keep warm. For filling combine ⅔ of the Rich Cream Sauce and next 4 ingredients in saucepan, mix. Add crab meat; warm. Prepare Hollandaise Sauce. Add wine to sauce, if desired; mix carefully. Spoon about ¼ cup of filling down center of each crêpe and roll up. Place in shallow baking pan. Place in slow oven (300°F.) to heat, 8 to 10 minutes. While heating; combine Hollandaise and remaining Rich Cream Sauce. Serve crêpes topped with Sauce. Yield: About 6 servings.

Sweet and Sour Pork

1 pound boneless lean pork shoulder, cut in 1-inch cubes
1 tablespoon shortening
1 can (8½ ounces) sliced pineapple
1 cup water
½ small onion, sliced and quartered
1 teaspoon salt
⅛ teaspoon pepper
⅓ cup sugar
⅓ cup vinegar
1 beef bouillon cube
1 sliver garlic
3 tablespoons cornstarch
1 tablespoon soy sauce
1 medium green pepper, cut in chunks
1 medium tomato, cut in thin wedges
3 cups hot cooked rice

Brown pork well in hot shortening in large skillet or Dutch oven over moderate heat. Turn meat pieces as needed to brown evenly. Saving syrup, drain pineapple. Combine syrup, ½ cup water, onion, salt and pepper. Pour over meat; cover and cook slowly until meat is fork tender, about 1 hour. Combine sugar, vinegar, remaining ½ cup water, bouillon cube, garlic, cornstarch and soy sauce in container. **STIR** (**2**) 2 seconds. Add to meat mixture. Cook stirring constantly until sauce is clear and thickened. Add quartered pineapple slices, green pepper chunks and tomato wedges. Heat to serving temperature. Serve immediately on hot rice. Yield: 4 servings.

Easy-Made Swiss Cheese Fondue

1¼ cups milk, scalded
1 pound Swiss cheese, Natural or processed, cut into ½-inch cubes
½ thin slice onion
¼ teaspoon salt
¼ teaspoon pepper
¼ teaspoon garlic salt
¼ teaspoon ground nutmeg
Dash of cayenne pepper
3 tablespoons flour
¼ to ⅓ cup dry white wine
French bread, cut or broken into bite-size pieces

Set blender speed at **CRUMB** (**3**). Pour hot milk into container. Cover. Start motor; add cheese cubes through top opening quickly, one at a time, processing until all cubes are added, 45 to 50 seconds. Add all but last 2 ingredients. **CRUMB** (**3**) just until smooth, 3 to 5 seconds. Pour into fondue dish, heavy saucepan or chafing dish over hot water. Cook slowly over very low heat, stirring constantly, until thickened. Stir in wine. Dip bread cubes into sauce using long handled fondue forks; twist to cover bread cubes with sauce. Yield: About 2¾ cups.

Blender Rarebit

1 cup milk, scalded
¾ pound Cheddar or American cheese, cut into ½-inch cubes
½ thin slice onion
½ teaspoon prepared mustard
¼ teaspoon Worcestershire sauce
Dash of cayenne pepper
3 tablespoons flour

Set speed at **MIX** (**7**) and pour hot milk into container. Start motor and add cheese cubes through **top opening,** quickly, one cube at a time, processing until all cubes are added, about 45 seconds. Add remaining ingredients in order listed. **MIX** (**7**) just until smooth, 3 to 5 seconds. Pour into heavy saucepan; cook slowly over very low heat, stirring constantly, until thickened. Serve on toast points as an entrée, as a dip, as a rich cheese sauce, etc. Yield: About 2 cups.

Beef-Vegetable Kabobs

See photo below (A)

Cut lean **boneless beef sirloin or tenderized round** into 1½ inch cubes. Marinate beef cubes generously in **Tomato French Dressing** (page 80) in covered container in refrigerator for several hours. Stir 2 or 3 times while marinating. Drain; save marinade. Thread meat cubes on skewers; broil 3 to 4 inches above a bed of low charcoal until ¾ done (rare, medium or well done). Turn skewers frequently to brown meat cubes evenly. Baste frequently with marinade or **Barbecue Sauce** (page 84). Remove cubes from skewers. Assemble meat, precooked **small potatoes, onions, zucchini** slices, or other cooked vegetables desired and **raw tomato wedges** and **green pepper squares.** Let guests thread their favorite foods onto skewers and heat, lightly browning them, 3 to 4 inches above a bed of low charcoal, to doneness desired. Baste often with marinade or Barbecue Sauce during heating.

Ham and Fruit Kabobs

See photo at left (B)

Cut **fully cooked ham** into 1½ inch cubes. Thread ham cubes, **fresh pineapple, peeled orange wedges** and **green pepper** squares onto skewers as desired. Brush well with **Honey Celery Seed Dressing** (page 80). Heat and lightly brown 3 to 4 inches above a bed of low charcoal, turning as needed to brown evenly, 8 to 10 minutes. Brush several times during heating with additional dressing.

Italian Meat Ball Dinner

1 pound ground beef, chuck, round or hamburger meat
1½ cups soft bread crumbs (page 100)
1 cup blender-grated Parmesan cheese (page 100)
½ cup milk
1 thin slice onion
2 teaspoons salt
¾ teaspoon oregano
¼ teaspoon pepper
1 can (1 pound 12 ounces) tomatoes
1 can (6 ounces) tomato paste
¾ cup (½-inch) sliced celery
1 medium onion, sliced and quartered
1 clove garlic, sliced
2 tablespoons flour
½ teaspoon sugar
2 tablespoons shortening
1 package (7 or 8 ounces) spaghetti, cooked and drained

Combine meat, crumbs and ¼ cup cheese in mixing bowl. Combine milk, onion, 1 teaspoon salt, ¼ teaspoon oregano, ⅛ teaspoon pepper in container. **STIR** (**2**) until well mixed, 3 to 4 seconds. Add to meat and mix well. Shape into balls using 1 rounded tablespoonful of meat per ball. Combine tomatoes, next 6 ingredients and remaining 1 teaspoon salt, ½ teaspoon oregano and ⅛ teaspoon pepper. **CRUMB** (**3**) until celery and onions are finely chopped, 5 to 10 seconds. Brown meat balls well in hot shortening in large skillet or Dutch oven over moderate heat, turning balls as needed to brown evenly. Pour sauce over meat balls and cook slowly until meat is thoroughly cooked and sauce thickened. Serve on hot seasoned spaghetti with remaining Parmesan cheese. Yield: About 4 to 6 servings.

A — Sweet 'N Sour Sauce (page 50)
B — Herb Butter (page 93)
C — Tartar Sauce (page 82)
D — Cheese Sauce (page 81)
E — Barbecue Sauce (page 84)
F — Bearnaise Sauce (page 83)
G — Charcoal Broiled Burgers (page 49)
H — Sweet 'N Sour Spareribs (page 50)
I — Charcoal Broiled Lobster Tails (page 48)
J — Charcoal Broiled Chuck Steak (page 48)

Tuna 'N Eggs in Casseroles

4 hard-cooked eggs, quartered
1 tablespoon lemon juice
1 teaspoon salt
1 recipe Quick White Sauce (Medium) (page 81)
2 cans (6½ or 7 ounces each) solid pack tuna, drained and coarsely flaked
½ cup buttered cereal crumbs (page 8)

Add 4 egg quarters to container. Set speed at **LO** (**1**) and then switch motor on and off quickly 2 times to coarsely chop egg. Empty into bowl; repeat 3 times. Stir lemon juice and salt into sauce. Add eggs and tuna; mix carefully. Spoon into 6 buttered individual casseroles. Sprinkle crumbs around edge of each. Heat to serving temperature in moderate oven (350°F.), 15 to 20 minutes. Yield: About 6 servings.

Sausage Tetrazzini

2 cups milk
3 tablespoons flour
1 teaspoon salt
¼ teaspoon pepper
1 small onion, sliced and quartered
¼ cup butter or margarine
1 can (10½ ounces) condensed cream of mushroom soup
¼ cup sherry, optional
1 can (4 ounces) sliced mushrooms, drained
1 package (7½ or 8 ounces) noodles, cooked, drained and salted
1 pound fully-cooked smoked sausage links or frankfurters, cut into ¼-inch slices
¾ cup blender-grated Parmesan cheese (page 100)
2 tablespoons diced pimiento

Combine first 5 ingredients in container, **STIR** (**2**) until onions are coarsely chopped, 5 to 8 seconds. Pour into large saucepan and add butter or margarine and soup. Place over low heat and cook until smooth and thickened. Add sherry, mushrooms, noodles, ½ of sausage slices and ½ of cheese. Mix and pour into shallow 2-quart casserole. Bake in moderate oven (350°F.) 20 minutes. Top with remaining sausage pieces and cheese. Garnish with pimiento pieces. Return to oven to bake until hot and bubbly, about 15 minutes. Yield: About 6 servings.

SALMON 'N EGGS IN CASSEROLES—Follow recipe for Tuna 'N Eggs In Casseroles (at left) and substitute **1 can** (1 pound) **salmon,** drained, skinned, boned and coarsely flaked for tuna. Yield: About 6 servings.

Baked Stuffed Whole Fish

1¼ cups ½-inch celery slices
1 medium onion, sliced and quartered
Cold water
1 quart (4 cups) coarse dry bread crumbs (page 100)
¼ cup lemon juice
2 1-inch squares of lemon peel (yellow part only), cut into quarters
2½ teaspoons salt
½ cup dairy sour cream
½ cup melted butter or margarine
1 3 or 4 pound dressed whole fish (whitefish, pike, bass, trout or red snapper)
Tartar Sauce (page 82)

Combine celery and onion in container; cover with cold water. **STIR** (**2**) just until vegetables at top travel down to blades. Stop motor at once and empty into sieve. Drain vegetables well. Add to bread crumbs. Combine lemon juice, rind and 1 teaspoon salt in container. **PUREE** (**4**) until lemon rind is finely chopped. Add lemon mixture, sour cream and ¼ cup butter or margarine to crumbs. Mix lightly. Sprinkle remaining 1½ teaspoons salt over inside and outside of fish. Stuff fish loosely with bread mixture. Close opening with small skewers or wooden picks. Place fish in large shallow well-greased baking pan. Brush with butter or margarine. Bake in moderate oven (350°F.) until fish flakes easily when tested with fork, 45 to 50 minutes. Brush fish several times during baking with butter or margarine. Remove skewers; serve with Tartar Sauce. Yield: About 6 servings.

Cheese and Bacon Strata

12 slices day old bread, crusts trimmed off
1 pound (16 slices) pasteurized process American cheese
2½ cups milk
4 eggs
1½ teaspoons Worcestershire sauce
1 thin slice onion
1 teaspoon prepared mustard
½ teaspoon salt
¼ teaspoon pepper
6 slices bacon, cut in half crosswise, fried crisp and drained

Top each bread slice with a cheese slice. Cut remaining cheese slices in half. Arrange ½ of the bread slices in bottom of well buttered large shallow casserole (11¾ x 7½ x 1¾ inches). Combine remaining ingredients in container except cheese and bacon; **STIR** (**2**) until well mixed 2 to 4 seconds. Cover bread slices with ½ of milk mixture. Arrange remaining bread slices on top of first layer. Drizzle remaining milk mixture over all. Set casserole in pan of shallow hot water. Bake in slow oven (325°F.) until set, 55 to 60 minutes. Remove from oven, top with remaining cheese and bacon. Return to oven to melt cheese. Let stand 5 minutes before cutting. Yield: 6 servings.

Crispy Baked Chicken

See photo on front cover

3 cups corn flakes
1¼ cups Blender-Made Mayonnaise (page 79)
1 thin slice onion
1½ teaspoons salt
1¼ teaspoons paprika
1 teaspoon seasoned salt
¼ teaspoon pepper
1 frying chicken (3 to 3½ pounds), cut into serving pieces

Set speed at **STIR** (**2**); add ½ cup corn flakes to container then turn switch on and off as many times as needed to coarsely chop crumbs for coating chicken, about 2 times. Empty container; repeat as necessary. Combine next 6 ingredients in container. **PUREE** (**4**) just until onion is finely chopped, 2 to 3 seconds. Spread chicken pieces with mayonnaise mixture. Cover; refrigerate 1 hour, if possible. Coat chicken pieces with crumbs. Arrange in oven proof skillet. Bake in moderate oven (375°F.) until chicken is fork tender, about 1 hour. Serve and keep warm on buffet server. Yield about 4 servings.

Chicken or Turkey And Ham Parmesan

1 recipe Rich Cream Sauce (Thick) (page 81)
½ cup milk
1 thin slice onion, quartered
½ teaspoon salt
½ teaspoon paprika
¼ teaspoon nutmeg
2 cans (3 ounces each) sliced mushrooms, drained
6 slices boiled ham
6 slices cooked chicken or turkey
½ cup blender-grated Parmesan cheese (page 100)

Combine sauce, milk, onion, salt, paprika and nutmeg in container. Set speed at **STIR** (**2**) then switch motor on and off until onion is finely chopped, 4 to 5 times. Stir in mushrooms. Arrange ham and chicken or turkey slices and sauce in layers in shallow 1½ quart baking dish. Sprinkle cheese over top. Bake in moderate oven (375°F.) until hot and bubbly and cheese browns. About 25 minutes. Yield: 6 servings.

Beef Rump Roast With Barbecue Sauce

4 to 5 pound rolled beef rump roast
3 tablespoons shortening
⅓ cup wine or cider vinegar
½ cup catsup or chili sauce
1 teaspoon liquid smoke, optional
2 teaspoons salt
1 clove garlic, quartered
1 small onion, sliced and quartered
1 stalk celery, cut in ½-inch lengths
1 cup water
Barbecue Sauce (page 84)

Brown meat well on all sides in hot shortening in heavy Dutch oven with heatproof handles, turning meat as needed to brown evenly. Combine remaining ingredients, except Barbecue Sauce in container. **PUREE** (**4**) until ingredients are finely chopped, 5 to 10 seconds. Pour over roast. Cover and place in moderate oven (350°F.) and cook until fork tender, about 2½ hours. Baste several times during roasting and turn meat at end of first hour of cooking. Slice and serve as an entrée or on buns with Barbecue Sauce. Yield: About 8 generous servings.

Chicken or Turkey Tetrazzini

Follow recipe for Sausage Tetrazzini (page 56) and make the following changes. Decrease onion to ½ small onion and substitute **1 pound cooked chicken or turkey,** cut into bite-size pieces, for sausage. Put all poultry pieces into spaghetti mixture. Proceed as for Sausage Tetrazzini. Yield: About 6 servings.

Hearty Sausage Lasagne

2 packages (8 ounces each) hard or cotto salami
1 can (1 pound) tomatoes
1 can (6 ounces) tomato paste
1 2-inch onion, sliced and quartered
½ cup sliced (½-inch) celery
4 sprigs parsley (no stems)
2 teaspoons basil
1½ teaspoons oregano
1½ teaspoons salt
2 dashes Tabasco sauce
¼ pound bacon, cut into 1-inch pieces
½ pound lasagne noodles, cooked and drained
1 pound sliced ricotta or drained large curd cottage cheese
1 package (6 ounces) sliced Mozzarella cheese
¾ cup Blender-Grated Parmesan cheese (page 100)

Cut 6 slices of sausage meat in quarters and save for topping casserole. Cut remaining sausage into ¾ inch squares. Add sausage pieces to container; set speed at **PUREE** (**4**) then turn switch on and off as needed to finely chop, 5 or 6 times. Empty container. For sauce combine next 9 ingredients in container. Set speed at **PUREE** (**4**) then switch motor on and off just until onion is coarsely chopped, 3 or 4 times. Pour into saucepan and add chopped sausage. Bring to simmering stage over low heat; cover and let simmer 20 minutes to blend flavors. Fry bacon pieces until crisp; drain. Stir bacon drippings into sauce. Spread ⅓ of the sauce over bottom of shallow 2-quart casserole. Layer ½ each of noodles, ricotta or cottage cheese, Mozzarella cheese slices and ⅓ of Parmesan cheese. Repeat layers of sauce, noodles, and cheeses. Top with remaining sauce, reserved salami pieces and sprinkle with remaining Parmesan cheese. Bake in moderate oven (350°F.) until thoroughly heated, 35 to 40 minutes. Yield: 6 to 8 servings.

Beef Stroganoff

2 pounds lean sirloin steak, sliced 1-inch thick
2 large Bermuda onions, quartered and sliced
Cold water
⅓ cup butter or margarine
1½ teaspoons salt
¼ teaspoon pepper
⅓ cup catsup
1 cup hot water
2 beef bouillon cubes
1 tablespoon Worcestershire sauce
½ pound fresh mushrooms, cleaned and sliced or 2 cans (4 ounces each), drained
1 tablespoon cornstarch
2 tablespoons cold water
1 cup dairy sour cream
8 servings hot cooked buttered and seasoned rice or noodles

Chill meat well. It will cut easier if chilled in freezer 20 minutes. Cut meat into pieces 1½ x 1 x ¼ inches. Chop onions as follows. Fill container ⅓ full with onion pieces; cover with cold water. Set speed at **LO** (**1**), turn motor on and off 2 or 3 times, or just until onion is very coarsely chopped. Stop motor at once and pour into sieve. Repeat process as needed. Brown meat in butter or margarine over moderate heat, stirring as needed to brown evenly. Add well drained onion, salt and next 5 ingredients; mix. Cover and cook slowly until meat is almost tender, about 25 minutes. Add mushrooms; cover and cook until soft. Mix cornstarch and water; stir into meat mixture and cook until starch is cooked, about 10 minutes. Blend in sour cream. Serve on rice or noodles. Yield: 8 servings.

Turkey or Chicken Divan

2 packages (9 ounces each) frozen asparagus spears, cooked and drained
1 recipe Cheese Sauce (Medium) (Page 81)
8 to 10 slices cooked turkey or chicken
4 slices pasteurized process American cheese, cut in half
⅓ cup buttered cereal crumbs (page 8)

Arrange asparagus in bottom of shallow baking dish and cover with ½ of sauce. Top with turkey or chicken slices. Cover with cheese slices and remaining sauce. Sprinkle crumbs over top. Bake in hot oven (425°F.) until heated and lightly browned, about 25 minutes. Yield: 6 servings.

Ham and Asparagus au Gratin

2 cups corn flakes
2 cups diced (¾-inch) cooked ham
1 recipe Rich Cream Sauce (Medium) (page 81)
2 5-inch green onions, in 1-inch lengths
1 tablespoon prepared mustard
½ teaspoon salt
¼ teaspoon pepper
2 packages (9 ounces each) frozen cut asparagus, cooked and drained
1 package (8 ounces) sliced process American or pimiento cheese, cut in half

Measure ½ cup corn flakes into container at a time. Set speed at **PUREE** (**4**); then switch motor on and off, until flakes are coarsely chopped, 3 to 4 times. Empty container after each processing. Repeat process with cooked ham. Combine ½ cup hot Rich Cream Sauce, onion, mustard, salt and pepper in container; **STIR** (**2**) just until onion is finely chopped, 3 or 4 seconds. Pour into sauce and add ham. Sprinkle ½ of flakes over bottom of well buttered 2 quart shallow oblong baking dish. Top with ½ of asparagus; pour ½ of sauce over asparagus; cover with ½ of cheese slices. Repeat with another layer of asparagus, cheese slices and sauce. Sprinkle remaining crumbs over top. Bake in moderate oven (350°F.) until hot and bubbly, 25 to 30 minutes. Yield: 6 servings.

Skillet Barbecued Pork Chops

6 rib pork chops 1-inch thick
1 tablespoon shortening
½ teaspoon salt
½ cup Honey Celery Seed Dressing (page 80)
1 cup Barbecue Sauce (page 84)
⅓ cup water

Brown chops well on both sides in hot shortening in large skillet; turning chops as necessary to brown evenly. Pour off excess fat. Season chops with salt. Mix remaining ingredients; pour over chops. Cover and cook slowly until chops are fork tender, about 1 hour. Serve with hot cooked rice, if desired. Yield: 6 chops, 4 to 6 servings.

Eggs Benedict

2 English muffins, split, toasted and buttered
4 slices grilled Canadian bacon or boned rolled ham
4 broiled (¼-inch) tomato slices
4 poached eggs or hot, sliced, hard-cooked eggs
1 recipe Hollandaise Sauce (page 84)

Quickly top each hot, toasted, English muffin half with a hot meat and tomato slice. Top with a poached egg or hard-cooked egg slices. Top with Hollandaise Sauce. Serve at once. Yield: 4 servings.

Plain Omelet

6 eggs
⅓ cup milk or half and half (half milk half cream)
½ teaspoon salt
⅛ teaspoon pepper
2 tablespoons butter or margarine

Combine first 4 ingredients in container; set speed at **STIR** (**2**) then switch on and off 3 or 4 times until well mixed. Melt butter or margarine in skillet or chafing dish over direct, but low, heat. Pour egg mixture into pan. Run a spatula around edge of pan during cooking, lift omelet slightly to let egg flow underneath. Crease omelet in center when eggs are soft cooked on top and fold in half. Serve. Yield: 3 to 4 servings.

Fancy Strawberry Omelet

Follow recipe for **Plain Omelet** (above) and decrease milk or half and half to ¼ cup and add **1 tablespoon sugar.** Separate eggs and **STIR** (**2**) egg yolks with milk 1 to 2 seconds. Whip egg whites with hand or electric beater until they form soft peaks. Fold into omelet mixture. Bake as directed for Plain Omelet. Just before folding omelet in half spread with ⅓ **cup thick strawberry jam**; fold and dust top with **confectioners' sugar.** Yield: 3 to 4 servings.

FLAMING STRAWBERRY OMELET — Prepare **Fancy Strawberry Omelet** (above) and pour slightly heated **rum or kirsch** over folded omelet in pan; ignite and serve when flame dies down.

Creamy Curried Shrimp

Creamy Curried Shrimp

See photo at left

Prepare **2 cups Curry Sauce** (page 81). Add **2 cups cooked cleaned shrimp**; heat well. Serve with **hot fluffy rice** and accompaniments desired, **chopped peanuts, flaked coconut, raisins, watermelon pickles,** and additional curry powder. Yield: 6 servings.

Chicken, Turkey or Pork Curry

1 recipe Curry Sauce (page 81)
¼ cup drained chutney
2 pieces preserved ginger, cut in half, optional
½ teaspoon salt
⅓ cup flaked coconut
1½ cups diced cooked chicken, turkey or pork
Hot cooked rice, toast points or patty shells

Combine Curry Sauce, chutney, ginger and salt in container. Set speed to **LO** (**1**) then turn switch on 2 or 3 times until chutney is coarsely chopped. Pour into saucepan; add coconut and poultry or pork. Heat. Serve on hot cooked rice, toast points or heated patty shells. Yield: About 3½ cups, about 6 servings.

Crab Newburg

1½ cups half and half (half milk half cream) or milk
3 egg yolks
3 tablespoons flour
¾ teaspoon salt
½ teaspoon paprika
¼ teaspoon pepper
¼ cup butter or margarine
1 pound crabmeat, shell and cartilage removed, diced
3 tablespoons sherry, optional
Hot buttered toast points or patty shells

Combine first 6 ingredients in container. **STIR** (**2**) until smooth, 3 to 4 seconds. Pour into heavy saucepan and add butter or margarine. Place over very very low heat and cook slowly until thick and smooth, stirring constantly, or cook in top of double boiler. Add crabmeat and heat. Remove from heat; stir in sherry if desired. Serve at once on toast points or in patty shells. Yield: About 3 cups, 6 servings.

South-Of-The-Border Eggs

½ pound bacon, cut in 1-inch pieces
¾ cup tomato sauce
¼ cup water
1 clove garlic, quartered
3 5-inch green onions, in 1-inch slices
¼ cup 1-inch green pepper squares
½ teaspoon chili powder
1 teaspoon salt
1 large tomato, washed, stemmed and diced
8 eggs
¼ cup milk, half and half (half milk half cream) or cream
3 tablespoons bacon drippings
Toast or tortillas, if desired

Pan fry bacon until crisp; drain and save drippings. Keep bacon warm. For sauce; combine next 6 ingredients and ½ teaspoon salt in container. Set speed at **STIR** (**2**) then turn switch on and off until onion and pepper are coarsely chopped, about 3 to 5 times. Pour into saucepan and add diced tomato. Simmer gently to blend flavors, about 8 to 10 minutes. Combine eggs, milk and remaining salt in container; **STIR** (**2**) 2 or 3 seconds to mix. Heat bacon drippings in fry pan. Add egg mixture; cook over moderate heat stirring gently during cooking. If desired, pile on hot toast or tortillas and top with sauce and bacon pieces. Yield: About 4 servings.

Scrambled Eggs

½ cup milk or half and half (half milk half cream)
6 eggs
1 teaspoon salt
⅛ teaspoon pepper
2 tablespoons butter or margarine

Combine first 4 ingredients in container. **STIR** (**2**) just until well mixed, about 3 to 4 seconds. Melt butter or margarine in fry pan over moderate heat, or in chafing dish over direct flame. Cook egg mixture, stirring gently, until cooked to desired doneness. Yield: 3 to 4 servings.

BRUNCH EGGS WITH POTATOES — Brown 1 package (9 ounces) frozen **French fries** in **2 tablespoons butter or margarine** over moderate heat. Season potatoes to taste with salt and pepper and pour egg mixture over potatoes. Cook as directed for Scrambled Eggs (above). Yield: 3 to 4 servings.

Salmon and Macaroni, Italian Style

1 can (1 pound) tomatoes
1 sliver garlic
2 teaspoons oregano
1 teaspoon salt
¼ teaspoon rosemary (optional)
¼ cup flour
1 cup milk
1 cup coarse dry-chopped onion (page 9)
¼ cup butter or margarine
1 package (7 or 8 ounces) elbow macaroni or rotini, cooked (about 4 cups, when cooked)
1 can (3 or 4 ounces) sliced mushrooms, drained
½ cup blender-chopped natural Cheddar cheese (page 100)
1 can (1 pound) salmon, drained, skinned, boned and flaked
¼ cup blender-shredded Parmesan cheese (page 100)
¼ cup buttered cereal or bread crumbs (page 8)

Combine tomatoes, garlic, oregano, salt, rosemary and flour in container. **STIR** (**2**) until well mixed, about 5 to 8 seconds. Pour into saucepan; stir in milk and add onions and butter or margarine. Cook slowly, stirring constantly, until mixture thickens. Combine sauce, macaroni, mushrooms, Cheddar cheese and salmon; mix carefully. Pour into shallow 2-quart baking dish. Mix Parmesan cheese and crumbs; sprinkle over top of casserole. Bake in moderate oven (350°F.) until well heated, about 30 minutes. Yield: About 6 servings.

Green Noodles Romana

½ pound green noodles
¼ cup cooking or olive oil
1 clove garlic, quartered
6 sprigs parsley (no stems)
1 teaspoon sweet basil
⅛ teaspoon pepper
½ cup blender-grated Parmesan cheese (page 100)

Cook noodles as directed on package label. Drain well and keep warm. Combine next 5 ingredients in container; **PUREE** (**4**) just until parsley is minced, 2 to 5 seconds. Turn into frypan; add noodles and heat slowly. Add cheese and toss. Yield: About 3 cups or 2 servings.

Pasta In Italian Meat Sauce

2 cans (10½ ounces each) tomato puree
1 large Bermuda onion, quartered and sliced
1 clove garlic, sliced
1 teaspoon sugar
1 teaspoon salt
½ teaspoon oregano
¼ teaspoon pepper
½ pound ground beef
2 tablespoons shortening
½ of 7 or 8 ounce package shell or elbow macaroni, cooked and drained
½ cup blender-grated Parmesan cheese (page 100)

Combine first 7 ingredients in container. Set speed at **STIR** (**2**) then switch motor on and off until onions are coarsely chopped, 5 to 8 times. Cook beef in hot shortening in large frypan until grey in color. Add tomato mixture and macaroni; mix. Cover and cook slowly until mixture is thickened; stir in macaroni. Sprinkle with Parmesan cheese before serving. Yield: About 4 to 6 servings.

Noodle Casserole Smetane

½ cup diced (¼-inch) Parmesan cheese
⅔ cup corn flakes
2 tablespoons melted butter or margarine
1 cup dairy sour cream
2 5-inch green onions in 1-inch lengths
1 package (6 or 6½ ounces) wide noodles, cooked, drained and salted
1 recipe Quick White Sauce (Medium) (page 81)
1 cup large curd cottage cheese, undrained

Add Parmesan cheese to container. **GRATE** (**6**) to fineness desired, about 15 seconds. Empty into small bowl. Pour corn flakes into container. Set speed at **PUREE** (**4**) then turn switch on and off as needed, 3 or 4 times or until flakes are crushed to size desired for crumb topping. Pour into small bowl; mix with melted butter or margarine. Add sour cream and onion to container. **PUREE** (**4**) until onions are finely chopped, 3 to 4 seconds. Stop motor and push ingredients into blades with rubber spatula, if necessary. Combine noodles, sauce, sour cream mixture and ½ of Parmesan and cottage cheese; mix and pour into 2 quart shallow baking dish. Spoon remaining cottage cheese over top. Edge casserole with corn flake crumbs and sprinkle with remaining Parmesan cheese. Bake in moderate oven (350°F.) until well heated and bubbly around edges, 45 to 50 minutes. Yield: 6 servings.

Chocolate Peppermint Stick Pie

1 quart vanilla ice cream
*1 cup chopped peppermint sticks or candy canes**
9-inch Fancy Edge Chocolate Wafer Crust (page 66)
Fudge Sauce (page 85)

Spoon ⅓ of ice cream into Fancy Edge Chocolate Wafer Crust. Sprinkle ⅓ of the chopped candy evenly over ice cream. Repeat 2 times. Place in freezer to harden. Serve plain or with Fudge Sauce. Yield: 1 9-inch pie, 8 servings.

*To chop peppermint sticks or candy canes (page 9) break candy into ½ or 1-inch lengths. Add 2 or 3 sticks or canes to container, one at a time. Set speed at **STIR** (**2**) then switch motor on and off as needed to chop candy moderately fine, 2 to 4 times, or as desired.

Fudge-Nut Sundae Pie

⅔ cup shelled peanuts, cashews, pecan or walnut halves
1 quart vanilla ice cream
9-inch Pecan Crumb Crust (page 64), chilled
1 cup Fudge Sauce (page 85), chilled

Pour nuts into container. Set speed at **STIR** (**2**) then turn switch on and off, as needed, until nuts are coarsely chopped (see page 100). Empty nuts into bowl. Quickly spoon ½ of ice cream into chilled crust; drizzle ½ of sauce over ice cream and sprinkle with ½ of nuts. Repeat. Freeze until firm, 4 to 5 hours. Yield: 1 9-inch pie; about 8 servings.

MOCHA PIE—Follow recipe for Fudge-Nut Sundae Pie (page 63) and substitute **coffee ice cream** for vanilla and use a **Cereal Crumb Crust** (page 65). Yield: 1 9-inch pie, about 6 to 8 servings.

Pecan Crumb Crust

10 graham crackers, quartered
½ cup pecan halves
¼ cup butter or margarine, melted
3 tablespoons sugar

PUREE (4) ⅓ of the graham crackers at a time until finely crumbed, about 10 seconds. Pour into bowl. Add pecans to container. Set speed at **STIR (2)** then turn switch on and off until nuts are finely chopped (see page 100), about 8 seconds. Add to crumbs. Add butter or margarine and sugar; mix. Pack evenly over bottom and up sides of 9-inch pie plate. Heat in moderate oven (350°F.) 5 minutes. Chill. Yield: One 9-inch crust.

PECAN CRUMB CRUST (8-INCH)—Proceed as for 9-inch crust (above) and use **7 graham crackers, ⅓ cup pecan halves, 3 tablespoons butter or margarine** and **2 tablespoons sugar.**

WHEAT GERM CRUMB CRUST—Follow recipe for Pecan Crumb Crust (above) and substitute **½ cup wheat germ** for pecans for 9-inch crust and **⅓ cup wheat germ** for pecans for 8-inch crust.

Pumpkin Pie

1½ cups undiluted evaporated milk
2 eggs
1½ cups canned pumpkin
1 cup sugar
¾ teaspoon salt
1¼ teaspoons cinnamon
½ teaspoon each of ground cloves, allspice, nutmeg and ginger
1 9-inch unbaked pastry shell

Combine ingredients, except crust, in container in order listed. **MIX (7)** 20 seconds; stop motor and stir with rubber spatula. **MIX (7)** 30 seconds, or until smooth. Pour into pie shell. Bake in hot oven (425°F.) 15 minutes; reduce heat to moderate (350°F.) and bake until knife inserted in center comes out clean, 35 to 40 minutes. Cool. Yield: 1 9-inch pie.

Lemon Ginger Pie

1⅓ cups cold milk
1 package (3¾ ounce) lemon instant pudding
1 cup whipped dessert topping
9-inch Gingersnap Crumb Crust (page 66)

Pour milk into container; add instant pudding. **STIR (2)** 10 seconds or until thoroughly mixed. Pour into bowl; fold in whipped dessert topping. Spoon into crust. Chill thoroughly. Serve plain or topped with additional whipped dessert topping. Yield: 1 8-inch pie, 5 to 6 servings.

QUICK LEMON CREAM PIE—Follow recipe for Lemon Ginger Pie (above) and substitute a **Fancy Brown Edge Cookie Crust** (page 66) and top with a layer of whipped cream or dessert topping. Garnish with **lemon slices,** if desired.

Strawberry Cheese Pie

See photo at right

¼ cup milk
2 eggs
1½ teaspoons vanilla
1 package (8 ounces) room temperature cream cheese, cubed
1½ teaspoons flour
¼ teaspoon salt
1 cup sugar
1 9-inch Graham Cracker Crumb Crust (page 66)
¼ cup water
2 pints strawberries, cleaned and ⅓ of berries cut in half
2 tablespoons cornstarch

For filling: Combine first 6 ingredients and ¼ cup sugar in container. **PUREE (4)** until smooth, 30 to 40 seconds. Stop motor; push ingredients into blades, as needed. Pour into Graham Cracker Crumb Crust. Bake in moderate oven (350°F.) until filling is set, about 20 minutes. Chill. For glaze: Add water, berry halves, remaining sugar, and cornstarch in container. **STIR (2)** until smooth, about 5 seconds. Pour into saucepan; cook slowly, stirring constantly, until clear. Stand whole berries, stem end down, on pie. Spoon warm glaze over berries. Chill. Yield: 1 9-inch pie, 6 to 8 servings.

Cereal Crumb Crust

*6 cups corn flakes**
⅓ cup butter or margarine, melted
3 tablespoons sugar

Add 1 cup of cereal to container at a time. Set speed at **PUREE** (**4**) and process until finely crumbed, about 5 seconds. Pour into bowl. Repeat. Add butter or margarine and sugar; mix well. Pack evenly over bottom and up sides of 9-inch pie plate. Heat in moderate oven (350°F.) 5 minutes. Chill. Yield: One 9-inch crust.

*Whole wheat or bran flakes may be substituted for corn flakes, if desired.

CEREAL CRUMB CRUST (**8-INCH**) — Proceed as directed for 9-inch Cereal Crumb Crust (above) but use 4½ **cups cereal flakes,** ¼ **cup butter or margarine** and **2 tablespoons sugar.**

Speedy Cherry Cream Pie

1¾ cups chilled milk
1 package (3¾ ounces) vanilla instant pudding mix
9-inch Vanilla Wafer Crumb or Fancy Brown Edge Cookie Crust (page 66)
1 can (1 pound) cherry pie filling
Whipped cream or dessert topping, if desired

Pour milk into container. Add pudding mix. **STIR** (**2**) until smooth and well mixed, about 10 seconds. Pour into crust at once. Chill. Top with cherry pie filling; chill until vanilla cream is firm enough to cut. Serve plain or with whipped cream or dessert topping, as desired. Yield: 1 9-inch pie, 6 servings.

BLUEBERRY CREAM PIE — Follow recipe for Speedy Cherry Cream Pie (above) and substitute **blueberry** for cherry **pie filling.**

Strawberry Cheese Pie

Graham Cracker Crumb Crust (9-inch)

*18 graham crackers, quartered**
⅓ cup butter or margarine, melted
3 tablespoons sugar

PUREE (4) ¼ of the graham cracker pieces at a time until finely crumbed, 10 to 15 seconds. Pour into bowl. Repeat until all crackers are crumbed. Add remaining ingredients; mix well. Pack crumbs evenly over bottom and sides of 9-inch pie plate. Heat in moderate oven (350°F.) 5 minutes. Chill. Yield: 1 9-inch crust.

*About 1⅓ cups crumbs

GRAHAM CRACKER CRUMB CRUST (8-inch)—Use **13 or 14 graham crackers, ¼ cup butter or margarine** and **2 tablespoons sugar.** Proceed as for 9-inch crust (above).

VANILLA WAFER CRUMB CRUST (9-inch)—Use **35 vanilla wafers** instead of graham crackers and proceed as for 9-inch Graham Cracker Crumb Crust (above). See photo page 63.

VANILLA WAFER CRUMB CRUST (8-inch)—Use **24 vanilla wafers** instead of graham crackers and proceed as for 8-inch Graham Cracker Crumb Crust (above).

GINGERSNAP CRUMB CRUST (9-inch)—Use **24 gingersnaps** instead of graham crackers and proceed as for 9-inch Graham Cracker Crumb Crust (above).

Fancy Brown Edge Cookie Crust

See photo page 63

24 brown edge cookies
¼ cup butter or margarine, melted
2 tablespoons sugar

Reserve 11 or 12 perfect cookies. Trim a ¼ inch edge off bottom of each cookie to make it stand straight in pie plate. Save cookies and trimmings. Break remaining untrimmed cookies in half. Proceed as directed for Cinnamon Graham Wafer Crust (page 69). Yield: 1 9-inch crust.

FANCY EDGE CHOCOLATE WAFER CRUST—Proceed as directed for Fancy Brown Edge Cookie Crust (at left) and substitute **thin chocolate cookie wafers** for brown edge cookies.

Apricot Pineapple Buttermilk Pie

2 cups buttermilk
¼-inch slice unpeeled orange, quartered
3 eggs
¼ cup thick pineapple preserves
1 teaspoon lemon extract or vanilla
¾ cup sugar
½ cup flour
½ teaspoon salt
9-inch unbaked pastry shell with high rim
1 can (1 pound) peeled apricot halves
4 teaspoons cornstarch
¼ cup pineapple preserves

Combine buttermilk and orange in container. **PUREE (4)** until orange rind is finely chopped, 5 to 6 seconds. Add next 6 ingredients to container. **STIR (2)** until mixed, 3 to 4 seconds. Pour into saucepan; cook slowly over very low heat, stirring constantly, until mixture thickens. (Or cook in top of double boiler, if preferred.) Bake pastry shell in hot oven (400°F.) 5 minutes. Reduce temperature to moderate oven (350°F.) and pour buttermilk mixture into shell. Bake until done, about 45 minutes. When done a metal knife inserted ½ inch deep in center of pie will come out clean. Cool on rack. Saving syrup; drain apricots very well on paper toweling. Pour syrup into cup and add water as needed to make 1 cup liquid. Mix cornstarch and ¼ cup liquid; add to remaining ¾ cup liquid. Cook sauce slowly, stirring constantly until clear and thickened. Stir in remaining preserves. Place well dried apricots, hollow side down on pie; drizzle sauce over fruit. Chill. Yield: 1 9-inch pie, 6 to 8 servings.

Chiffon Mincemeat Pie

⅓ cup orange juice
1½ envelopes (1½ tablespoons) unflavored gelatin
1¼ cups boiling water
½ cup sugar
2 ¼-inch slices unpeeled orange, quartered
1½ cups prepared mincemeat
2 to 4 tablespoons brandy, optional
2 cups whipped cream or dessert topping
9-inch Vanilla Wafer Crumb or Fancy Brown Edge Cookie Crust (page 66)

Pour orange juice in container; add gelatin and let stand 5 minutes. Add boiling water and **STIR** (**2**) until gelatin is dissolved, about 4 to 5 seconds. Add sugar and orange pieces and **STIR** (**2**) until orange rind is finely chopped, 5 to 10 seconds. Add mincemeat and **STIR** (**2**) just until well blended, 3 to 5 seconds. Pour into bowl; chill until mixture starts to thicken. Fold in brandy and whipped cream or dessert topping. Spoon into crust. Chill. Yield: 1 9-inch pie, 6 to 8 servings.

Custard Pie

2¼ cups milk
4 eggs
½ cup sugar
½ teaspoon salt
1 teaspoon vanilla
9-inch unbaked pastry shell
Nutmeg

Combine first 5 ingredients in container. Turn speed to **LO** (**1**) and mix just until blended, 3 to 5 seconds. Pour into pastry shell. Sprinkle with nutmeg. Bake in hot oven (400°F.) until filling is set, 35 to 40 minutes or until a metal knife inserted ½ inch deep in center of filling comes out clean. Cool on rack. Yield: 1 9-inch pie, 6 to 8 servings.

MINCEMEAT CUSTARD PIE—Follow recipe for Custard Pie (above). Substitute **lemon extract** for vanilla and omit nutmeg. Spread **1 cup prepared mincemeat** evenly over unbaked crust and pour **custard mixture** over top. Bake as directed for custard pie.

COCONUT CUSTARD PIE—Follow recipe for Custard Pie (above). Omit nutmeg and sprinkle **½ cup flaked coconut** over filling before baking.

Peanut Brittle Ice Cream Pie

3 pints slightly softened vanilla ice cream
1 cup very well-chilled applesauce
1¼ cups blender-chopped peanut brittle (page 9)
1 well-chilled 9-inch Graham Cracker Crumb Crust (page 66)
1 cup whipped cream or dessert topping

Chill large mixing bowl in freezer. Combine ice cream, applesauce and ¾ cup candy in bowl; mix quickly. Return to freezer to harden slightly. Pack mixture into pie shell. Return to freezer to harden. Just before serving, edge pie with whipped cream or dessert topping and sprinkle with remaining candy. Yield: About 8 servings.

Grape-Nuts Walnut Pie

1 cup milk, half and half (half milk half cream) or undiluted evaporated milk
½ cup light or dark corn syrup
3 eggs
¼ cup melted butter or margarine
¾ cup (packed) brown sugar, broken-up
¼ cup flour
¼ teaspoon salt
1 teaspoon vanilla
⅔ cup walnut halves
½ cup grape-nuts
9-inch unbaked pastry shell
Whipped cream or dessert topping

Combine first 8 ingredients in container; **STIR** (**2**) just until well mixed, 4 to 5 seconds. Add nuts; set speed to **STIR** (**2**) then switch motor on and off 2 or 3 times or until nuts are coarsely chopped. Add grape-nuts, with speed at **STIR** (**2**) turn motor on and off immediately. Pour into pastry shell. Bake in moderate oven (350°F.) until done, about 1 hour. Cool. Serve plain or topped with whipped cream or dessert topping, if desired. Yield: 1 9-inch pie, 6 servings.

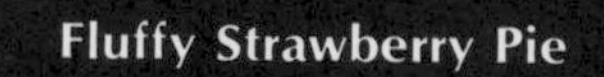

Fluffy Strawberry Pie

Frozen Lime Pie in Chocolate Coconut Crust

Double Chocolate Pie (page 70)

Frozen Lime Pie in Chocolate Coconut Crust

See photo at left

1 envelope (1 tablespoon) unflavored gelatin
½ cup lime juice
⅓ cup boiling water
4 thin unpeeled slices (⅛-inch) fresh lime, quartered
1 can (15 ounces) sweetened condensed milk
1 package (3 ounces) room temperature cream cheese, cubed
3 tablespoons sugar
¼ teaspoon salt
1½ teaspoons lemon extract
3 to 5 drops green food color, or as desired
2 cups whipped cream or dessert topping
9-inch Chocolate Coconut Crust (page 70)
Chocolate curls, optional

Sprinkle gelatin over lime juice in container. Let stand 5 minutes. Add boiling water; **STIR (2)** 5 seconds or until gelatin is melted. Add lime slices; process at **MIX (7)** until peel is finely chopped, about 25 seconds. Add next 4 ingredients; **MIX (7)** until smooth, about 25 seconds. Pour into bowl; stir in lemon extract and green color to tint a pretty green color. Chill until syrupy. Fold in whipped cream or dessert topping. Pour into chocolate crust. Freeze. Garnish with chocolate curls, if desired. Yield: 1 9-inch pie, 8 to 10 servings.

Cinnamon Graham Wafer Crust

See photo page 63

32 long single cinnamon graham cracker wafers
3 tablespoons butter or margarine, melted
2 tablespoons sugar

Select 19 perfect wafers. Cut ¼ inch from each wafer (or the amount required to make the wafers the length to stand upright around edge of a 9-inch pie plate); save wafers and trimmings. Break remaining wafers in half. Crumb trimmings and broken wafers, ⅓ at a time, in container by processing at **PUREE (4)** until finely crumbed, 10 to 15 seconds. Repeat 2 times. Combine crumbs, butter or margarine and sugar; mix. Stand reserved wafers upright around edge of pie plate and press crumb mixture over bottom. Chill well. Yield: 1 9-inch crust.

Fluffy Strawberry Pie

See photo at left

1 package (3 ounces) strawberry flavored gelatin
1 cup boiling water
1 package (10 or 12 ounces) frozen strawberries, partially defrosted and cubed
½ teaspoon vanilla
2 egg whites
⅓ cup sugar
9-inch Cinnamon Graham Wafer Crust (recipe at left)
Few drops of red food color, optional
Strawberries and mint for garnishing pie, optional

STIR (2) gelatin and hot water in container until gelatin is dissolved, about 3 to 5 seconds. Add strawberries and vanilla to container and **STIR (2)** until strawberries are finely chopped, about 5 seconds. Pour into mixing bowl. Chill until consistency of egg whites. **Watch carefully, mixture will set quickly.** Beat egg whites with rotary or electric beater until they form soft peaks. Add sugar gradually and beat until egg whites are stiff and glossy. Fold into gelatin mixture. Tint, a pretty pink, if desired, with food color. Spoon into crust; chill until set. Garnish, if desired, with strawberries and mint. Yield: 1 9-inch pie, 6 to 8 servings.

Southern Pecan Pie

½ cup half and half (half milk half cream), cream or undiluted evaporated milk
⅔ cup dark corn syrup
3 tablespoons melted butter or margarine
3 eggs
1½ teaspoons vanilla
¾ cup sugar
3 tablespoons flour
¼ teaspoon salt
1¼ cups pecan halves
9-inch unbaked pie shell
Whipped cream, or dessert topping, optional

Combine first 8 ingredients in container; **STIR (2)** just until mixed, about 2 seconds. Add nuts; set speed at **STIR (2)** then switch motor on and off just until nuts are very coarsely chopped, 2 or 3 times. Pour into pie shell. Bake in moderate oven (350°F.) 45 minutes or until filling is puffed and crust browned. Cool. Serve plain or with topping, if desired. Yield: 1 9-inch pie, 6 to 8 servings.

Peanut Brittle Butterscotch Pie

¾ cup peanuts
¼ cup cold water
1 envelope (1 tablespoon) unflavored gelatin
1 package (3½ or 4 ounce) butterscotch pudding and pie filling mix (not instant)
2 cups milk
1 cup finely broken peanut brittle
1 cup whipped cream or dessert topping
9-inch Graham Cracker Crumb Crust (page 66)

Add peanuts to container; set speed at **STIR** (**2**) then switch motor on and off just until nuts are coarsely chopped, 2 or 3 times (see page 100). Pour into bowl and save. Pour cold water into container; add gelatin; let stand 5 minutes. Prepare pudding with 2 cups of milk as directed on package label. Pour hot pudding into container; **CRUMB** (**3**) until gelatin is melted, about 15 seconds. Cool in bowl until mixture starts to thicken. While pudding is cooling add candy to container, ½ cup at a time; set speed at **STIR** (**2**) then switch motor on and off until candy is chopped moderately fine. Fold candy and whipped cream or dessert topping into pudding. Spoon into pie shell; sprinkle top with chopped peanuts. Chill until firm. Serve plain or with additional whipped cream or dessert topping. Yield: 1 9-inch pie, 6 to 8 servings.

Jiffy Banana Cream Pie

1⅓ cups chilled milk
1 package (3¾ ounce) vanilla or butterscotch flavored instant pudding
2 cups whipped dessert topping
2 small bananas, sliced
9-inch Fancy Brown Edge, Chocolate or Vanilla Cookie Crust (see page 66)

Pour milk into container. Add pudding. **STIR** (**2**) until well mixed, about 10 seconds. Pour into bowl and fold in 1 cup whipped dessert topping. Pour ⅓ of pudding into crust, top with a layer of sliced bananas; repeat. Spread remaining pudding over top. Cover with remaining 1 cup whipped topping. Chill. Yield: 1 9-inch pie, 6 servings.

JIFFY CHOCOLATE BANANA CREAM PIE—Follow recipe for Jiffy Banana Cream Pie (above) and substitute **1 package** (**4½ ounce**) **chocolate flavored pudding mix** for vanilla or butterscotch.

Chocolate Coconut Crust For Frozen Pies

See photo page 63

2 squares unsweetened chocolate, cut into small pieces
2 tablespoons milk
2 tablespoons butter or margarine
½ cup sifted confectioners' sugar
1½ cups shredded or flaked coconut

Press a sheet of aluminum foil over bottom and sides of 9-inch pie plate allowing a 1-inch overhang around plate. **STIR (2)** chocolate, switching motor on and off until finely grated. Combine milk and butter or margarine; scald. Pour over chocolate. Process at **LO (1)** until chocolate is melted, about 5 seconds. Add sugar; process at **LO (1)** until mixed. Stop motor; push mixture into blades with rubber spatula as needed. Add ½ cup coconut; process as directed for sugar. Turn into bowl; mix in remaining coconut. Press mixture in even layer over bottom and sides of pie plate. Freeze. Carefully lift crust in foil from plate. Peel off foil and slide crust into buttered pie plate. Freeze and fill. Yield: One 9-inch crust.

Double Chocolate Pie

See photo page 68

1 envelope (1 tablespoon) unflavored gelatin
¼ cup cold water
1 package (3½ to 4 ounces) chocolate pudding and pie filling (not instant)
2 cups milk
1 package (6 ounces) semi-sweet chocolate bits
1½ teaspoons vanilla
2 cups sweetened whipped cream or dessert topping
9-inch Fancy Brown Edge Cookie Crust (page 66)

Sprinkle gelatin over water in blender container; let stand 5 minutes. Prepare chocolate pudding and pie filling with milk as directed on package label. Empty chocolate bits into container. Add hot pudding; turn to **LO** (**1**) until chocolate and gelatin melt, and mixture is smooth, about 20 seconds. Pour into bowl and cool stirring frequently, until mixture starts to thicken. Fold in vanilla and whipped cream or dessert topping. Spoon into Fancy Brown Edge Cookie Crust. Chill until set. Serve with whipped cream or dessert topping, if desired. Yield: 1 9-inch pie, 6 to 8 servings.

Preserves and Relishes

Orange Marmalade

See photo at right

*¾ cup orange and lemon rind slivers**
*1 cup orange and lemon rind squares**
Cold water
1½ cups hot water
⅛ teaspoon soda
*2½ cups orange and lemon pieces**
5 cups sugar
½ of 6 ounce bottle liquid fruit pectin
**About 3 medium oranges and 1 lemon are needed to prepare this amount of rind and pieces.*

Wash oranges and lemons. Remove rind from oranges in quarters or sixths. Lay rind flat on cutting board; shave off white fiber. Use a sharp knife or scissors and prepare ¾ cup very fine orange and lemon rind slivers, about 1-inch long. Turn into saucepan. Cover with water; simmer 5 minutes. Pour off liquid; repeat process with same rind and save. Prepare 1 cup orange and lemon rind squares. Place in container and add ½ cup cold water. **CHOP** (**8**) uncooked rind by turning switch on and off as needed to coarsely chop. Drain; discard liquid and empty rind into large 4½ to 5 quart saucepan. Add 1½ cups hot water and soda. Bring to a boil; cover and simmer 20 minutes. Prepare fruit pieces while rind is simmering. Trim all white membrane from oranges and lemon and cut each into eighths. **CHOP** (**8**) orange and lemon pieces, 1 cup of fruit at a time, by turning switch on and off as needed to coarsely chop. Empty into large saucepan with rind. Add drained slivered, cooked rind and sugar; mix well. Bring to a fast rolling boil; boil hard for 1 minute, stirring constantly. Remove from heat and stir in pectin immediately. Skim if necessary. Cool about 5 minutes; stir and ladle into jars. Cover with hot paraffin. Yield: About 5 cups.

Cranberry Orange Relish

See photo page 71

1 medium unpeeled seedless orange
1 cup sugar
⅛ teaspoon ground cloves, optional
2 cups washed cranberries

Peel orange; save ¼ of the peeling and cut it into strips ¼-inch wide and 1-inch long. Cut orange into eighths. **CHOP** (**8**) orange, orange rind, ½ cup sugar and cloves, if used, 15 seconds or until rind is chopped. Add 1 cup cranberries and remaining sugar. **STIR** (**2**) 10 seconds or until cranberries are coarsely chopped; add remaining cranberries and **STIR** (**2**) 10 seconds or until coarsely chopped. Pour into covered container; Chill thoroughly. Yield: About 1¾ cups.

Strawberry or Raspberry Jam

See photo page 71

2 packages (10 or 12 ounces) frozen strawberries or raspberries, partially defrosted and cubed
1 tablespoon lemon juice
2½ cups sugar
½ of 6 ounce bottle liquid fruit pectin

CHOP (**8**) 1½ packages of berries in container, ½ package at a time, by turning switch on and off just until berries are coarsely chopped. Pour into 4½ to 5 quart saucepan or Dutch oven. Add unchopped berries, lemon juice and sugar. Bring to a full rolling boil and boil hard 1 minute, stirring constantly. Remove from heat; stir in pectin. Skim off any foam on surface. Stir and skim 5 minutes. Ladle into sterilized jars. Cover with paraffin. Yield: About 4½ cups.

Peachy Apricot Jam

See photo page 71

1 cup dried apricots
2 cups hot water
2 packages (10 ounces each) frozen sliced peaches, partially defrosted and separated
4 cups sugar
⅓ cup lemon juice
1 bottle (6 ounces) liquid fruit pectin

Cook apricots in water until puffed. Save ⅓ cup liquid and drain. **CHOP** (**8**) apricots, the reserved liquid and ½ of the peaches in the container by switching motor on and off as needed, until coarsely chopped. Empty into 4½ to 5 quart saucepan or Dutch oven. Stir in sugar and lemon juice. Bring to a full rolling boil and boil hard 1 minute, stirring constantly. Remove from heat, stir in pectin. Skim off any foam. Cool 5 minutes, stirring gently. Ladle into sterilized jars. Cover with paraffin. Yield: About 5½ cups.

Corn Relish

2 cups cider vinegar
1 cup sugar
4 teaspoons dry mustard
2 tablespoons salt
¼ teaspoon pepper
1 tablespoon celery seed
2 cups thinly sliced cabbage
2 medium onions, sliced
2 green peppers, cleaned, cut into 1-inch squares
1 small red pepper, cleaned, cut into 1-inch squares
Cold water
6 cups well-drained cooked or canned whole kernel corn

Combine first 6 ingredients in large saucepan or Dutch oven. Heat. While mixture is heating prepare vegetables. Combine ⅓ of the cabbage, onion and peppers in container. Cover with very cold water. **CHOP** (**8**) just until vegetables at top travel down to blades. Empty into sieve, at once, drain well and add to vinegar mixture. Repeat process 2 times to chop remaining vegetables. Add corn. Cook slowly, about 45 minutes, stirring frequently. Ladle into sterilized jars and seal at once. Yield: About 4 pints.

Frozen Fruit Salad

Frozen Fruit Salad

See photo at left

1 can (1 pound 14 ounces) fruit cocktail, drained
1 can (1 pound 4 ounces) pineapple chunks, drained
2 cups miniature marshmallows
16 maraschino cherries, whole
½ cup pecan halves, whole
1 package (8 ounce) room temperature cream cheese, cubed
½ cup Blender-Made Mayonnaise (page 79)
¼ cup confectioners' sugar
1 thin slice unpeeled orange, quartered
2 cups whipped cream or dessert topping
Red food color, as desired

Combine first 5 ingredients in mixing bowl; mix carefully and chill. **BLEND** (**10**) next 4 ingredients 10 seconds. Stop motor; push ingredients into blades with rubber spatula. **BLEND** (**10**) until smooth, about 10 seconds. Pour over fruits; mix. Fold in whipped cream or dessert topping. Tint, as desired with red food color. Spoon into aluminum foil lined 9 x 5 x 3 inch loaf pan. Freeze. Unmold and slice. Serve on salad greens with Blender-Made Mayonnaise. Yield: About 8 cups. 10 to 12 servings.

Frozen Cranberry Salad

½ cup Blender-Made Mayonnaise (page 79)
1 package (8 ounce) room temperature cream cheese, cubed
½ cup confectioners' sugar
3 to 4 drops red food color
1 can (8¾ ounces) crushed pineapple
1 cup canned whole cranberry sauce
1 cup whipped cream or dessert topping

GRATE (**6**) first 4 ingredients and syrup from pineapple 30 seconds, or until smooth. Turn into bowl, add remaining ingredients; mix carefully. Spoon into aluminum foil lined 8½ x 4½ x 2⅝ inch loaf pan. Freeze. Unmold, slice and serve on lettuce leaves. Yield: About 4½ cups, 6 servings.

Sour Cream Potato Salad (page 77)
Avocado Mousse
Salad Greens with Bacon Dressing

Salad Greens with Bacon Dressing

See photo at left

8 cups torn salad greens
8 slices crisp bacon, crumbled
⅓ cup bacon drippings
1 thin slice unpeeled lemon, quartered
¼ cup vinegar
1 tablespoon sugar
1 teaspoon prepared mustard
½ teaspoon salt
2 5-inch green onions, in 1-inch pieces
2 hard-cooked eggs, quartered
Freshly ground pepper

Combine salad greens and bacon in mixing bowl; chill. **GRATE** (**6**) next 7 ingredients 15 seconds, or until finely chopped. Add eggs; **STIR** (**2**) 3 to 4 seconds, or until eggs are coarsely chopped. Pour into saucepan; heat. Pour over greens; sprinkle with pepper. Toss lightly; serve at once. Yield: About 6 cups, 6 to 8 servings.

SPINACH SALAD WITH BACON DRESSING — Follow recipe for Salad Greens with Bacon Dressing (above). Use **8 cups torn spinach leaves** (no stems) in place of salad greens. Yield: About 6 cups, 6 to 8 servings.

Avocado Mousse

See photo at left

2 packages (3 ounces each) lime flavored gelatin
1 cup boiling water
½ inch slice unpeeled lime, quartered
½ cup cold water
6 ice cubes (or 1 cup ice water)
1 large avocado, peeled, seeded and sliced
¾ cup Blender-Made Mayonnaise (page 79)
1 cup dairy sour cream

MIX (**7**) first 2 ingredients 10 seconds, or until gelatin is dissolved. Add next 3 ingredients; **MIX** (**7**) 20 seconds, until lime is finely chopped. Add avocado and mayonnaise. **MIX** (**7**) 15 seconds, or until smooth. Pour into bowl; fold in sour cream. Turn into 5½ cup oiled mold. Chill until firm. Unmold, garnish with assorted fruits and mint sprigs, if desired. Yield: About 5½ cups, 6 to 8 servings.

Orange Cranberry Mold

2 cups fresh cranberries
⅔ cup cold water
1 medium orange, unpeeled and diced
1 stalk celery, in 1-inch pieces
2 packages (3 ounces each) lemon flavored gelatin
1 cup boiling water
1½ cups sugar
3 ice cubes (or ½ cup ice water)

MIX (**7**) cranberries and ⅓ cup cold water 10 seconds, or until coarsely chopped. Pour into mixing bowl. **MIX** (**7**) orange, celery and remaining ⅓ cup cold water 10 seconds, or until coarsely chopped. Stop motor; push ingredients into blades, if needed. Add to bowl. **MIX** (**7**) gelatin and boiling water 10 seconds, or until dissolved. Add sugar; **MIX** (**7**) 5 seconds; add ice cubes and **MIX** (**7**) 15 seconds. Pour over cranberry mixture; stir. Chill until mixture begins to set. Pour into 8-cup mold. Chill until firm. Unmold on salad greens. Yield: 8 cups, 10 to 12 servings.

Fruity Whipped Gelatin

1 package (3 ounces) fruit flavored gelatin
1 cup boiling water
3 ice cubes (or ½ cup ice water)
1 can (1 pound) fruit cocktail, drained
½ cup miniature marshmallows

MIX (**7**) gelatin and boiling water 10 seconds, or until gelatin is dissolved. Add ice cubes; **MIX** (**7**) 10 seconds. Pour into bowl. Mix in drained fruit cocktail and marshmallows. Chill until mixture starts to set. Pour into oiled 5 cup mold or 8 x 8 x 2 inch pan. Chill until firm. Serve as salad or dessert. Yield: 5 cups, 4 to 6 servings.

Pineapple-Cucumber Salad Mold

½ cup cold water
1 medium cucumber, unpeeled and sliced
1 stalk celery, in 1-inch slices
1 can (1 pound 4½ ounces) crushed pineapple, undrained
2 packages (3 ounces each) lime flavored gelatin
1 cup boiling water
3 ice cubes (or ½ cup ice water)
1 package (8 ounce) room temperature cream cheese, cubed
¾ cup Blender-Made Mayonnaise (page 79)
2 drops green food color

MIX (**7**) first 3 ingredients 20 seconds, or until finely chopped. Pour into mixing bowl; stir in pineapple. **MIX** (**7**) gelatin and boiling water 10 seconds, or until gelatin dissolves. Add ice cubes or ice water; **MIX** (**7**) 5 seconds. Add cream cheese, mayonnaise and color. **WHIP** (**5**) 10 seconds, or until smooth. Pour over cucumber mixture; mix. Chill until syrupy. Pour into 7½ cup oiled mold. Chill until firm. Unmold on salad greens; garnish with fruits, shrimp or tuna chunks, as desired. Yield: About 7½ cups, 10-12 servings.

LEMON-PINEAPPLE CHEESE RING — Follow recipe for Pineapple Cucumber Salad Mold above. Substitute **lemon** for lime **gelatin;** omit cucumber and celery. Substitute **¾ cup milk** for the cold water. Pour into 7 cup oiled ring mold. Chill until firm. Yield: About 7 cups; 10-12 servings.

Chicken, Turkey or Ham Salad

¼ cup Basic French Dressing (page 80)
2 cups diced cooked chicken, turkey or ham
1 cup sliced celery
½ cup Blender-Made Mayonnaise (page 79)
2 medium sweet pickles, in 1-inch slices
¼ teaspoon salt

Combine Basic French Dressing and poultry or ham; mix. Chill 1-2 hours. Add celery. **CRUMB** (**3**) remaining ingredients 7 seconds, or until smooth and pour over salad mixture; mix carefully. Serve as salad or use as sandwich filling. Yield: About 3 cups, 4 salad servings.

Tuna Salad

Follow recipe for Chicken, Turkey or Ham Salad at left; substitute **2 cans** (7 ounces each) **solid pack tuna,** drained and flaked, for poultry or ham. Add **1 thin unpeeled lemon slice, quartered,** with pickles when blending. Yield: About 4 cups, 4 to 6 servings.

Chicken or Turkey Salad Élégant

2 cups diced cooked chicken or turkey
1 can (5 ounce) water chestnuts, drained and sliced
1 can (11 ounce) mandarin orange sections, drained
1 cup halved seeded green grapes
1½ cups cooked rice, blanched and chilled
½ cup toasted slivered almonds
½ cup Blender-Made Mayonnaise (page 79)
1 thin slice unpeeled lemon, quartered
2 sprigs parsley (no stems)
½ teaspoon salt
1 teaspoon curry powder, optional
1 cup whipped cream or dessert topping

Combine first 5 ingredients and ¼ cup almonds in bowl; mix and chill. **GRATE** (**6**) next 5 ingredients 30 seconds, or until smooth. Add to salad mixture. Add whipped cream or dessert topping; mix. Serve on salad greens; sprinkle remaining almonds over top. Yield: About 6 cups, 8 to 10 servings.

Tuna Dinner Salad

4 cups Tuna Salad (above)
2 cups drained cooked elbow macaroni, chilled
½ cup diced Cheddar cheese
1 cup cooked peas, chilled
⅔ cup Blender-Made Mayonnaise (page 79)

Combine ingredients; mix carefully. Yield: About 6½ cups, 6 to 8 servings.

Vegetables Vinaigrette

½ cup cider or wine vinegar
½ cup sugar
⅓ cup water
⅓ cup salad oil
½ teaspoon salt
1 sliver garlic
3 5-inch green onions, in 1-inch slices
4 medium sweet pickles, in 1-inch slices
1 to 1½ pounds drained, cooked or canned vegetables (asparagus spears, green beans or carrot sticks)

STIR (**2**) first 8 ingredients 10 seconds, or until onions and pickles are finely chopped. Pour over vegetable desired. Cover; chill overnight. Drain vegetable. Leftover marinade may be refrigerated 2 or 3 days and re-used if desired. Yield: About 1¾ cups marinade; 4-6 servings Vegetables Vinaigrette.

Old Fashioned Coleslaw

4 cups sliced cabbage
4 5-inch green onions, in 1-inch slices
2 carrots, peeled and sliced
½ green pepper, diced
Cold water
⅓ cup vinegar
⅓ cup salad oil
¼ cup sugar
1 teaspoon salt
½ teaspoon celery seed
2 sprigs parsley (no stems)

Fill container loosely, ⅔ full, with mixture of cabbage, onions, carrots and green pepper. Add cold water to cover. **CHOP** (**8**) just until vegetables at top travel to blades, about 5 seconds. Empty into sieve; drain vegetables very well. Refill container; repeat process. Chill vegetables. **CRUMB** (**3**) remaining ingredients, 5 seconds, or until parsley is minced. Pour over drained vegetables; mix. Serve at once. Yield: About 3 cups, 4 to 6 servings.

Sour Cream Potato Salad

See photo on page 74

2 stalks celery, in 1-inch slices
12 small radishes, cut in half
1 small onion, sliced
Cold water
4 cups sliced, chilled, cooked potatoes
2 hard-cooked eggs, sliced
½ cup dairy sour cream
¾ cup Blender-Made Mayonnaise (page 79)
½ teaspoon celery seed
1¼ teaspoons prepared mustard
½ teaspoon seasoned salt
1½ teaspoons salt

Combine first 3 ingredients in blender container; cover with water. **GRATE** (**6**) just until vegetables at top travel down to blades, about 5 seconds. Empty container into sieve; drain vegetables well. Combine vegetables, potatoes and eggs in mixing bowl. **STIR** (**2**) remaining ingredients 10 seconds, or until smooth. Pour over potatoes; mix carefully. Yield: About 5½ cups, 6 to 8 servings.

3-Bean Salad

1 can (15½ ounces) cut green beans
1 can (15½ ounces) cut wax beans
1 can (1 pound) kidney beans
½ cup vinegar
½ cup salad oil
¼ cup water
8 medium sweet pickles in 1-inch slices
3 5-inch green onions, in 1-inch slices
2 stalks celery, in 1-inch slices
¼ green pepper, diced
½ cup sugar
1½ teaspoons salt

Drain beans; combine in refrigerator dish. **CRUMB** (**3**) remaining ingredients 15 seconds, or until coarsely chopped. Pour over beans. Mix; cover and marinate overnight. Yield: About 5½ cups, 6 to 8 servings.

Kidney Bean Salad

½ cup Blender-Made Mayonnaise (page 79)
1 stalk celery, thinly sliced
¼ green pepper, diced
1 recipe well drained 3-Bean Salad (above)

Combine ingredients; mix carefully. Serve on crisp salad greens. Yield: 6 cups, 6-8 servings.

Basic French Dressing (page 80)

Blender-Made Mayonnaise

Honey Celery Seed Dressing (page 80)

Avocado Pouring Dressing (page 80)

Salad Dressings

Blender-Made Mayonnaise

See photo at left

2 eggs
1 teaspoon dry mustard
1 teaspoon salt
1 teaspoon sugar
½ teaspoon paprika
¼ teaspoon celery salt
Dash of pepper or cayenne
⅓ cup lemon juice or vinegar
2 cups salad oil

CHOP (**8**) first 8 ingredients and ¼ cup oil 5 seconds. Add remaining oil in a fine steady stream through top opening while motor runs, about 60 seconds, or until thick and smooth. If necessary, stop motor and push ingredients into blades. Yield: About 2⅔ cups.

THOUSAND ISLAND DRESSING—STIR (**2**) **1 cup Blender-Made Mayonnaise** (above), **¼ cup chili sauce** and **½ thin onion slice** 20 seconds. Stop motor; add **2 medium sweet pickles,** in ½ inch slices, **8 stuffed olives** and **1 sliced hard-cooked egg. STIR** (**2**) 10 seconds or until ingredients are coarsely chopped. Yield: About 1¾ cups.

GREEN GODDESS DRESSING—Combine **1 cup Blender-Made Mayonnaise** (above), **½ cup dairy sour cream, ¼ cup parsley sprigs** (no stems), **1** (**5-inch**) **green onion** in 1-inch pieces, **4 anchovy fillets, 1 thin slice unpeeled lemon,** quartered, and **2 or 3 drops green food color** in container. **GRATE** (**6**) 20 seconds or until smooth. Yield: About 1⅔ cups.

MARMALADE DRESSING FOR FRUITS—CRUMB (**3**) **⅓ cup Blender-Made Mayonnaise** (above), **½ cup orange marmalade, 1 package** (**3 ounce**) **room temperature cream cheese,** cubed, **¼ inch slice unpeeled orange,** quartered, and **¼ teaspoon curry powder,** if desired, 40 seconds or until smooth. Pour into bowl; fold in **1 cup whipped cream** or **dessert topping.** Yield: About 2¼ cups.

WHIPPED FRUIT SALAD DRESSING—Combine **1 cup Blender-Made Mayonnaise** (left), **1 can** (**8¾ ounces**) **crushed pineapple,** drained, **1 thin slice unpeeled orange,** quartered and **2 pieces preserved ginger** in container. **STIR** (**2**) 10 seconds or until fruit is finely chopped. Pour into mixing bowl; fold in **1 cup whipped cream or dessert topping.** Yield: About 2½ cups.

ROQUEFORT OR BLUE CHEESE DRESSING — Combine **1 cup Blender-Made Mayonnaise** (left), **1 cup dairy sour cream** and **1 thin slice unpeeled lemon,** quartered, in container. **STIR** (**2**) 25 seconds or until smooth. Pour into bowl; add **1 package** (**3 or 4 ounces**) **Roquefort** or **blue cheese,** cubed, and mix. Yield: About 2¼ cups.

WATERCRESS SALAD DRESSING—GRATE (**6**) **1 cup Blender-Made Mayonnaise** (left), **½ bunch washed watercress leaves, ½ clove garlic,** sliced, and **½ inch square of lemon rind** 30 seconds or until watercress and rind are finely minced. Yield: About 1¼ cups.

BANANA CREAM DRESSING—Combine **¼ cup Blender-Made Mayonnaise** (left), **1 peeled banana** cut in 1-inch slices, **4 maraschino cherries, 2 tablespoons honey** or **sugar** and **1 thin slice unpeeled lemon,** quartered, in container. **CRUMB** (**3**) 15 seconds or until smooth. Fold in 1 cup whipped cream or dessert topping. Yield: About 2 cups.

Old Fashioned Cooked Salad Dressing

2 eggs
1 cup milk or water
⅓ cup sugar
3 tablespoons flour
1½ teaspoons salt
1½ teaspoons dry mustard
¼ teaspoon paprika
¼ inch slice unpeeled lemon, quartered
⅓ cup vinegar
1 cup dairy sour cream

WHIP (**5**) first 8 ingredients 10 seconds or until smooth. Pour into heavy saucepan; cook slowly over low heat, stirring constantly, until thickened. Stir in vinegar. Cool thoroughly; fold in sour cream. Yield: About 2¾ cups.

Pineapple Orange Dressing

1 package (8 ounce) room temperature cream cheese, cubed
¼ cup orange juice
¼ cup well drained pineapple tidbits or orange sections
2 tablespoons honey or sugar
1 thin slice unpeeled orange, quartered
1 thin slice unpeeled lemon, quartered
¼ teaspoon salt

BLEND (10) ingredients 10 seconds or until fruits are finely chopped. Yield: About 1⅓ cups.

Tomato French Dressing

1 can (10½ ounces) condensed tomato soup
½ cup cider or wine vinegar
½ cup salad oil
¼ cup sugar
1 tablespoon Worcestershire sauce
1 teaspoon salt
1 teaspoon dry mustard
1 thin slice onion
½ small clove garlic, sliced
2 dashes Tabasco sauce

CRUMB (3) ingredients 15 seconds or until smooth. Yield: About 2½ cups.

Fruit Cream Dressing

⅔ cup pineapple or orange juice
2 eggs
½ cup sugar
2 tablespoons cornstarch
½ teaspoon salt
¼ inch slice unpeeled orange, quartered
¼ inch slice unpeeled lemon, quartered
1 cup whipped cream or dessert topping

CHOP (8) first 7 ingredients 30 seconds, or until fairly smooth. Pour into heavy saucepan. Cook over low heat, stirring constantly, until thickened. Cool thoroughly. Fold in whipped cream or dessert topping. Yield: About 2 cups.

CONFETTI FRUIT DRESSING — **GRATE (6) 12 drained red or green maraschino cherries** 5 seconds, or until coarsely chopped. Fold into **Fruit Cream Dressing** (above). Yield: About 2 cups.

Basic French Dressing

See photo page 78

1 cup salad oil
¼ cup vinegar or lemon juice
¼ cup sugar
1 teaspoon dry mustard
1 teaspoon salt
1 teaspoon paprika
½ thin slice onion

CRUMB (3) ingredients 25 seconds or until onion is minced. Yield: About 1½ cups.

AVOCADO POURING DRESSING — *(see photo page 78)*, Combine Basic French Dressing ingredients (above) in container and add **1 peeled, pitted and diced avocado** and **¼ inch unpeeled lemon slice,** quartered. Turn to **HI (13)** for 20 seconds, or until smooth. If necessary, stop motor and push ingredients into blades with rubber spatula. Yield: About 2 cups.

ROQUEFORT POURING DRESSING — Prepare Basic French Dressing (above), pour into bowl. Stir in **⅓ to ½ cup crumbled Roquefort cheese.** Yield: About 1¾ cups.

GARLIC DRESSING—Combine Basic French Dressing ingredients (above) and **1 clove garlic,** sliced, in container. Blend as directed for French Dressing. Yield: About 1½ cups.

CELERY SEED DRESSING — Combine Basic French Dressing ingredients (above) in container and add **½ to 1 teaspoon celery seed** before blending. Yield: 1½ cups.

Honey Celery Seed Dressing

See photo page 78

¾ cup honey
¾ cup salad oil
½ cup sugar
½ cup lemon juice or vinegar
2 teaspoons prepared mustard
1½ teaspoons paprika
1 teaspoon celery seed
¾ teaspoon salt
½ thin slice onion

STIR (2) ingredients 20 seconds or until well mixed. Yield: About 2¼ cups.

Sauces

Quick White Sauce (Medium) for Creamed Dishes

See photo at right

2 cups milk
¼ cup flour
½ teaspoon salt
Dash of pepper
¼ cup butter or margarine

CRUMB (**3**) first 4 ingredients until smooth, about 10 seconds. Pour into saucepan; add butter or margarine. Cook, over low heat, stirring constantly, until smooth and thickened. Use for creaming vegetables, meats, poultry or fish or preparing scores of interesting sauces. Yield: About 2¼ cups.

THIN WHITE SAUCE FOR MAKING CREAM SOUPS — Follow above recipe; reduce flour and butter to 2 tablespoons each. Yield: About 2¼ cups.

THICK WHITE SAUCE FOR MAKING CROQUETTES — Follow recipe (above) for Quick White Sauce (Medium): increase both flour and butter or margarine to ⅓ cup each. Yield: About 2¼ cups.

RICH CREAM SAUCES — Follow recipes for White Sauces above (Thin, Medium or Thick) and substitute **half and half** (**half milk half cream**) for milk.

BECHAMEL SAUCE — Follow recipe (above) for Quick White (Medium) or Rich Cream Sauce (Medium); add a dash of **nutmeg** and, if desired, substitute **1 cup of meat stock or bouillon** for 1 cup of milk or cream.

CHEESE SAUCE — Add ½ **pound grated or chopped Cheddar cheese** and ½ **teaspoon prepared mustard** to 2¼ cups hot Quick White or Rich Cream Sauce (Medium) (above); stir until cheese melts. Yield: About 2¾ cups.

Quick White Sauce

CURRY SAUCE — Stir **1 to 2 teaspoons curry powder**, or to taste, into 2¼ cups hot Quick White Sauce or Rich Cream Sauce (Medium) (at left).

Spicy Sour Cream Sauce for Hot Dogs

1 cup (½ pint) dairy sour cream
⅓ cup Blender-Made Mayonnaise (page 79)
2 tablespoons prepared mustard
2 5-inch green onions, in 1-inch slices
2 teaspoons Worcestershire sauce
¼ teaspoon salt
2 dashes Tabasco sauce, optional

Combine ½ cup sour cream and remaining ingredients in container. Turn to **LO** (**1**) until onions are finely chopped, about 3 to 5 seconds. Stop motor; add remaining sour cream and push ingredients into blades. Turn to **LO** (**1**) and switch on and off as needed to mix. Delicious with hot dogs, smoked sausage links or cold cuts. Yield: About 1⅓ cups.

Steak or Burger Sauce

- *1 small onion, sliced*
- *1 stalk celery, in ½-inch slices*
- *¼ green pepper cleaned and sliced*
- *1 cup catsup*
- *½ cup water*
- *½ cup chili sauce*
- *1 tablespoon sugar*
- *½ teaspoon salt*
- *½ teaspoon liquid smoke*
- *¼ teaspoon pepper*

CRUMB (**3**) ingredients until vegetables are coarsely chopped, about 4 to 6 seconds. Pour into small saucepan. Simmer gently to blend flavors, 12 to 15 minutes. Delicious on barbecued or broiled steaks, burgers, chicken and ribs. Yield: About 2¼ cups.

Caper Sauce

- *1 cup Blender-Made Mayonnaise (page 79)*
- *1 tablespoon drained capers*
- *4 sprigs parsley (no stems)*

CRUMB (**3**) all ingredients 10 seconds. Yield: About 1 cup.

Sour Cream Mustard Sauce

- *1 cup (½ pint) dairy sour cream*
- *½ cup Blender-Made Mayonnaise (page 79)*
- *¼ cup prepared or Dijon mustard*
- *2 dashes Tabasco sauce*

Combine ingredients in container in order listed. Turn speed to **LO** (**1**) and switch motor on and off 2 or 3 times or until mixed. Push ingredients into blades with rubber spatula each time motor is stopped. Delicious with ham, corned beef and cold cuts. Yield: About 1½ cups.

Tartar Sauce

- *1 cup Blender-Made Mayonnaise (page 79)*
- *3 2-inch sweet pickles, in ½-inch slices*
- *1 5-inch green onion, in 1-inch slices or ⅙ of small onion, sliced*
- *3 sprigs parsley (no stems)*
- *1 thin slice unpeeled lemon, quartered*
- *1 tablespoon drained capers, optional*
- *1 teaspoon chervil, optional*

Combine ingredients in container. **STIR** (**2**) until pickles are coarsely chopped, about 10 seconds. Serve with fish or seafood. Yield: About 1¼ cups.

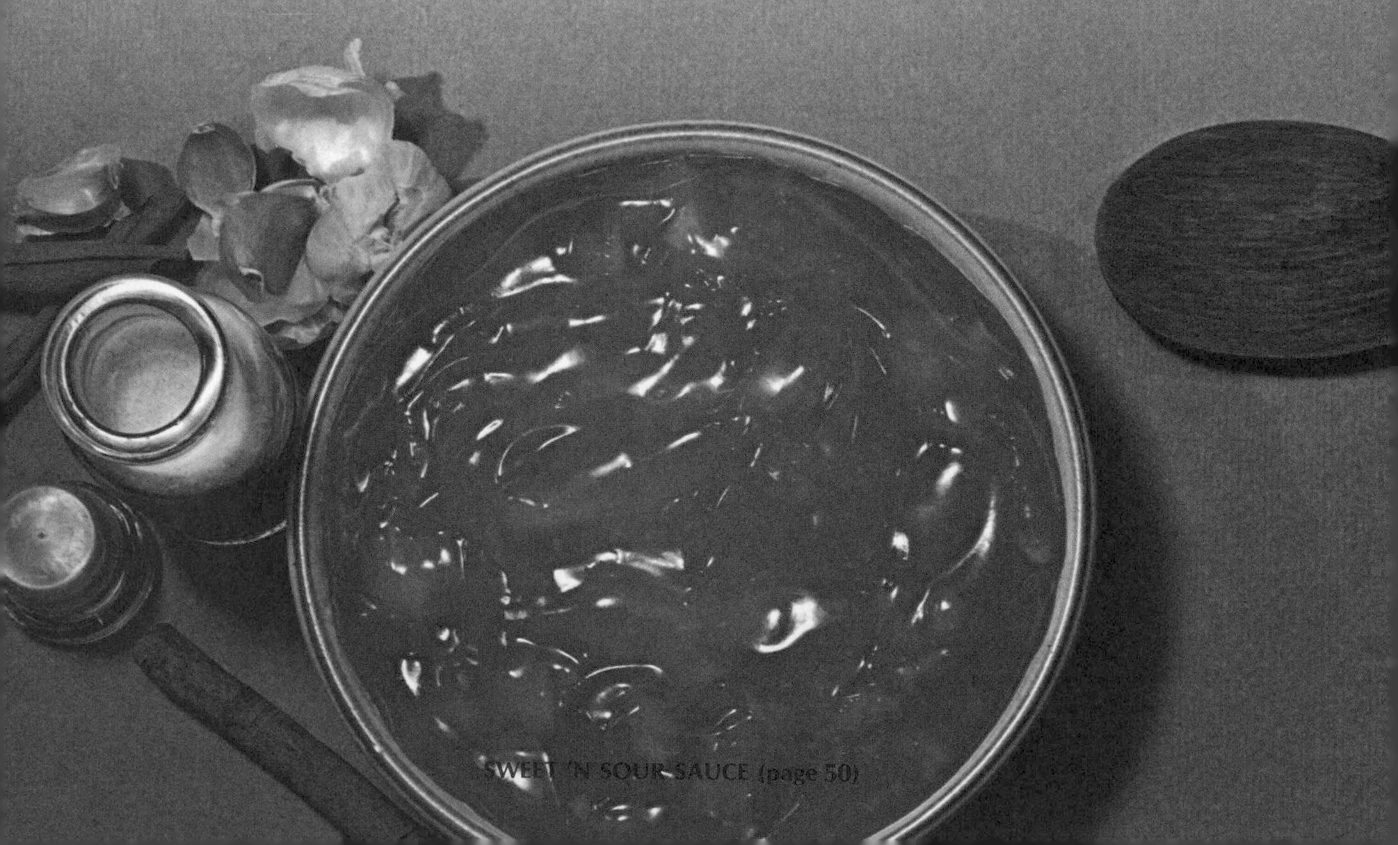

SWEET 'N SOUR SAUCE (page 50)

Hard Sauce

2 tablespoons half and half (half milk half cream)
⅓ cup soft butter or margarine
½ teaspoon vanilla, lemon or almond extract
1 cup confectioners' sugar

WHIP (**5**) first 3 ingredients until smooth, 3 or 4 seconds. Add ½ cup sugar and **CRUMB** (**3**) until smooth, 3 to 4 seconds. Add remaining sugar and **CRUMB** (**3**) until smooth, 3 to 4 seconds. Stop motor and push ingredients into blades with rubber spatula, as needed. Pile in serving dish and refrigerate until firm. Serve with plum, cranberry or other hot puddings or with fruit cake. Yield: About ¾ cup.

BRANDY HARD SAUCE—Follow Hard Sauce recipe (above) and substitute **2 tablespoons of brandy** for half and half and omit extracts. Serve on plum or suet puddings or with fruit cake.

Bearnaise Sauce

¼ cup water or dry white wine
3 tablespoons tarragon vinegar
1 thin slice onion
4 sprigs parsley (no stems)
Dash of salt
½ cup butter or margarine
3 egg yolks
½ cup Blender-Made Mayonnaise (page 79)

Combine first 5 ingredients in saucepan; simmer 5 minutes. Add butter or margarine and melt. **GRATE** (**6**) egg yolks 10 seconds. With motor running add hot liquids in fine stream and **GRATE** (**6**) 15 seconds. Pour into heavy saucepan; cook, stirring constantly, until thickened. Remove from heat and stir in mayonnaise. Serve with beef steak, roasts, or burgers. Yield: About 1⅔ cups.

ORANGE HARD SAUCE—Follow Hard Sauce recipe (page 83) and substitute **2 thin slices unpeeled orange,** cut into quarters for half and half and omit extracts. Serve on puddings, with fruit cake or on hot waffles.

Orange Sauce

3/4 cup orange marmalade
3/4 cup orange juice
3 1/4-inch unpeeled orange slices, quartered
2 or 3 large pieces preserved ginger or 1/2 teaspoon ground ginger
2 tablespoons cornstarch
2 tablespoons sugar
2 tablespoons vinegar
1/2 teaspoon salt
3/4 cup well-drained orange sections or seedless green grape halves
1/4 cup Cointreau, optional

CRUMB (**3**) first 8 ingredients in container until finely chopped, 2 to 4 seconds. Pour into saucepan and cook over low heat, stirring constantly, until thickened. Fold in orange sections or grapes and Cointreau, if used. Serve with roast pork, duck or ham, spareribs, pork chops, etc. Yield: About 2 1/2 cups.

Seafood Cocktail Sauce

1 1/4 cups chili sauce or catsup
2 teaspoons horseradish
1 thin slice onion
1/2 stalk celery, in 1-inch slices
1 thin slice unpeeled lemon, quartered

Combine ingredients in container. **CRUMB** (**3**) until celery and lemon are finely chopped, 10 to 12 seconds. Serve with chilled shrimp, crab or lobster. Yield: About 1 1/4 cups.

Hollandaise Sauce

1 cup butter or margarine
3 egg yolks
1/2 teaspoon salt
1/8 teaspoon pepper
1 tablespoon hot water
2 tablespoons lemon juice

Melt butter or margarine over hot water or in heavy saucepan over very low heat. Combine next 3 ingredients in container. **CRUMB** (**3**) 3 or 4 seconds. Turn to **BLEND** (**10**) and add hot water and lemon juice in fine stream, while motor is running, until mixed, about 3 seconds. Add butter or margarine in fine stream, while motor is running. Serve at once. Yield: About 1 1/3 cups.

Barbecue Sauce

See photo page 55

1 cup catsup
2 tablespoons oil
3 tablespoons vinegar
1 tablespoon Worcestershire sauce
3 tablespoons sugar
2 dashes Tabasco sauce
1 medium onion, sliced
2 drops liquid smoke, optional

CHOP (**8**) all ingredients until smooth, about 10 seconds. Heat slowly to blend flavors. Serve hot or cold on meats, poultry or fish or use as final basting sauce on barbecue ribs, chops, chicken, or burgers. Yield: About 1 3/4 cups.

Melba Sauce

1 package (10 ounces) frozen raspberries, partially defrosted and cubed
1/2 cup currant jelly
2 tablespoons cold water
1 tablespoon cornstarch

PUREE (**4**) ingredients by switching motor on and off just until ingredients are finely chopped. Push ingredients into blades with rubber spatula as needed when motor is stopped. Pour into saucepan and cook, stirring constantly, until clear and slightly thickened. Cool. Serve over fresh or cooked peach or pear halves, over fruit topped pound cake slices or atop pineapple, lemon or orange sherbet. Yield: About 1 1/2 cups.

Fudge Sauce

½ cup milk
½ cup confectioners' sugar
¼ cup light corn syrup
1 tablespoon butter or margarine
1 package (6 ounces) semi-sweet chocolate bits
½ teaspoon vanilla

Heat first 4 ingredients, in saucepan, slowly to simmering stage. Combine chocolate bits and vanilla in container, add very hot liquid; **CRUMB** (**3**) 10 seconds or until smooth. Serve warm, cold or at room temperature over ice cream or cake. Yield: About 1⅓ cups.

Peanut Fudge Sauce

1⅓ cups Fudge Sauce (above)
½ cup peanut butter

CRUMB (**3**) ingredients in container 15 seconds or until smooth. Serve on ice cream or cake. Yield: About 1⅔ cups.

Quick Strawberry Sundae Sauce

1 package (10 or 12 ounces) frozen strawberries, partially defrosted and cubed
3 tablespoons water
3 tablespoons sugar
1½ tablespoons cornstarch

Prepare as directed for Melba Sauce (page 84). Cool and serve atop ice cream, waffles, pancakes, crepés or cake slices. Yield: About 1¼ cups.

QUICK RASPBERRY SUNDAE SAUCE—Follow recipe for Quick Strawberry Sundae Sauce (above) and substitute **frozen raspberries** for strawberries. If desired, stir in 1 tablespoon **rum.** Serve on ice cream, cake, waffles or ice cream filled meringue shells.

Apricot Sundae Sauce

1 cup dried apricots
1 cup hot water
½ cup sugar
¼ inch slice unpeeled orange, quartered
½ cup light corn syrup

Simmer first 3 ingredients for 5 minutes. **CRUMB** (**3**) all ingredients 15 seconds or until fairly smooth. Chill. Serve on ice cream or cake slices. Yield: About 2 cups.

Butterscotch Dessert Sauce

1 package (6 ounces) butterscotch bits
½ cup milk
2 tablespoons sugar
¼ teaspoon salt
¼ teaspoon maple flavoring or ½ teaspoon vanilla

Empty bits into container. Heat milk, sugar and salt slowly to simmering stage. Pour over bits. **STIR** (**2**) until smooth, about 10 seconds. Add maple flavoring or vanilla and **STIR** (**2**) until blended, 2 to 3 seconds. Chill, stirring frequently. Serve on ice cream or cake. Yield: About ¾ cup.

BUTTERSCOTCH PECAN SAUCE — Stir **⅓ cup chopped pecans** into chilled Butterscotch Dessert Sauce (above). Yield: About 1¼ cups.

Choco-Toffee Sundae Sauce

12 chocolate covered toffee bars (¾ ounce each), broken into quarters
¼ cup milk or water
¼ teaspoon salt
¾ teaspoon vanilla

Place about ¼ cup of candy pieces, at a time, in container; cover and turn speed to **HI** (**13**) and switch motor on and off until candy is finely chopped. Empty candy into saucepan; add milk or water and salt. Heat slowly, stirring constantly until most of candy is melted. Stir in vanilla. Serve on ice cream or cake slices. Yield: About ¾ cup.

Creamy Vegetable
Bacon Soup

Soups

Fish Chowder

1 cup (¼-inch) carrot slices
1 cup diced (½-inch) raw potatoes
½ cup water
1 teaspoon salt
3 cups milk
3 tablespoons flour
¼ small onion, sliced
6 sprigs parsley (no stems)
3 tablespoons butter or margarine
¼ teaspoon rosemary
¼ teaspoon leaf thyme
1 cup flaked cooked fish (haddock, salmon, tuna or other fish)

Combine carrots, potatoes, water and ½ teaspoon salt in saucepan; cover and simmer until carrots are tender, about 15 minutes. **CRUMB (3)** next 4 ingredients and remaining ½ teaspoon salt 10 seconds or until onion is chopped. Pour into saucepan and cook slowly, stirring constantly, until smooth and thickened slightly. Add butter or margarine and stir until melted. Add herbs, vegetables and fish; heat and serve. Yield: About 5½ cups, 5 to 6 servings.

Cream of Carrot Soup

3 cups Thin White Sauce (page 81)
1½ cups drained, cooked, fresh or canned, sliced carrots
1 teaspoon salt
⅛ teaspoon pepper
Dash of nutmeg, if desired

Combine 1 cup sauce, carrots, salt, pepper and nutmeg, if used, in container. **STIR (2)** 25 to 30 seconds or until finely chopped. Pour into saucepan with remaining 2 cups sauce; heat and serve. Yield: About 4 cups, 4 to 6 servings.

CREAM OF ONION SOUP—Follow recipe for Cream of Carrot Soup (at left) and substitute **1½ cups well-drained, cooked, fresh or canned, small onions** for carrots, reduce salt to ½ teaspoon and omit nutmeg. **STIR (2)** 5 seconds or until coarsely chopped. Proceed as directed for Cream of Carrot Soup. Yield: About 3⅔ cups, 4 to 6 servings.

Asparagus Soup

1 pound fresh asparagus, washed, trimmed, cut in 1-inch pieces
¾ cup water
¼ cup flour
1½ teaspoons salt
⅛ teaspoon nutmeg
¼ cup butter or margarine
3 cups milk

Simmer asparagus in water in covered pan until tender, 8 to 10 minutes. Combine asparagus and liquid and next 3 ingredients in container. **GRATE (6)** 10 seconds, or until fairly smooth. Pour into saucepan; stir in butter or margarine and milk. Cook slowly, stirring constantly, until thickened. Yield: About 5 cups, 6 servings.

Creamy Vegetable Bacon Soup

See photo at left

1 package (10 ounces) frozen mixed vegetables
½ cup sliced (¼-inch) celery
3 cups milk
½ small onion, sliced
¼ cup flour
1½ teaspoons salt
¼ teaspoon pepper
¼ cup bacon drippings, butter or margarine, as desired
8 slices crisp fried bacon, broken into ½-inch pieces

Cook frozen vegetables and celery in water to cover until vegetables are tender; drain and keep warm. **STIR (2)** 1 cup milk and next 4 ingredients 15 seconds or until onion is finely chopped. Pour into heavy saucepan; add remaining 2 cups milk and bacon drippings, butter or margarine. Cook, stirring constantly, until hot and slightly thickened. Add cooked vegetables and bacon; heat and serve. Yield: About 4¾ cups, 4 to 6 servings.

HEARTY BURGER SOUP — Follow recipe for Creamy Vegetable Bacon Soup (page 87); make following changes. Increase onion to 1 small one and flour to ⅓ cup. Cook ½ **pound ground beef** slowly in 1 tablespoon butter or margarine until meat is grey in color. Add ⅓ **cup catsup** and cook until meat is crumbly and lightly browned; add to soup and mix well. Yield: About 5½ cups, 5 to 6 servings.

Curry Soup

½ small onion, sliced
2 celery stalks, in ¼ inch slices
¼ cup butter or margarine
3 tablespoons flour
1½ teaspoons curry powder
1 teaspoon salt
2 chicken bouillon cubes
3 cups milk
4 teaspoons flaked coconut, optional

Sauté onion and celery in butter or margarine until onion is tender; pour into container. Add flour, curry powder, salt, bouillon cubes and 1 cup milk. **GRATE (6)** 20 seconds, or until vegetables are finely chopped; pour into saucepan. Stir in remaining milk; cook until thickened, stirring constantly. Top each serving with 1 teaspoon coconut, if desired. Yield: About 3½ cups, 4 servings.

Vichyssoise

2 chicken bouillon cubes
½ cup hot water
½ teaspoon salt
½ teaspoon celery salt
½ small onion, sliced
4 servings hot instant mashed potatoes or 1⅔ cups hot mashed potatoes
2 cups milk
1 cup half and half (half milk half cream) or cream

PUREE (4) first 5 ingredients 15 seconds or until onion is finely chopped. Add potatoes and 1 cup milk. **PUREE (4)** 15 seconds or until smooth. Stop motor, push ingredients into blades with rubber spatula as needed. Stir in remaining 1 cup milk and half and half or cream. Chill well. Garnish servings with sour cream and chopped chives, if desired. Yield: About 5 cups, 6 to 8 servings.

Mulligatawny

1 medium apple, peeled and cubed
1 medium onion, sliced
1 medium carrot, in ½-inch slices
1 clove garlic, sliced
¼ cup butter or margarine
2 cups water
3 tablespoons flour
2 chicken bouillon cubes
1 teaspoon curry powder
1 teaspoon salt
½ cup half and half (half milk half cream)
1½ cups diced cooked chicken or turkey (about 7 ounces)

Sauté apple, onion, carrot and garlic in butter or margarine until onion is tender. **CRUMB (3)** water, flour, bouillon cubes, curry powder, salt and apple-vegetable mixture 20 seconds, or until smooth. Pour into saucepan. Cook, stirring constantly, until thickened. Stir in half and half and chicken or turkey; heat. Serve as soup or over cooked rice, if desired. Yield: About 4⅓ cups soup, 6 servings.

Quick Chicken or Turkey Corn Soup

1 cup diced, cooked, chilled or frozen chicken or turkey
1 can (1 pound) cream-style corn
1 can (10½ ounces) condensed cream of chicken soup
2 cups milk
½ teaspoon salt
1 tablespoon butter or margarine

STIR (2) chicken or turkey 2 to 3 seconds or until very coarsely chopped. Empty container; save chicken or turkey. **STIR (2)** corn and soup 5 to 8 seconds or until well mixed but not smooth. Pour into saucepan; stir in milk and salt. Heat, stirring frequently; add butter or margarine and allow to melt. Stir in chicken or turkey. Heat slowly; serve hot. Yield: About 5½ cups, 6 to 8 servings.

QUICK HAM AND CORN SOUP — Follow recipe for Quick Chicken or Turkey Corn Soup (above) and substitute **1 cup diced chilled cooked ham** for chicken or turkey. Yield: About 5½ cups, 6 to 8 servings.

Gazpacho

1 clove garlic, sliced
1 small onion, sliced
½ green pepper, cleaned and sliced
1½ cups chilled tomato juice
½ medium cucumber, peeled and sliced
2 medium tomatoes, peeled, seeded and quartered
1 teaspoon salt
¼ teaspoon pepper
½ cup chilled chicken bouillon (or 1 bouillon cube dissolved in ½ cup hot water and chilled)
2 tablespoons olive oil
3 tablespoons wine vinegar

CHOP (**8**) first 3 ingredients and ½ cup tomato juice 30 seconds or until very finely chopped. Add cucumber, tomatoes, salt and pepper. **CHOP** (**8**) 20 seconds or until ingredients are finely chopped, but not smooth. Pour into bowl. Stir in remaining 1 cup tomato juice, bouillon, oil and vinegar. Cover; chill well. Serve in small soup bowls in crushed ice. Garnish with watercress and cucumber slices or serve with an assortment of buttered croutons, diced cucumber, green pepper, onion and tomato, as desired. Yield: About 4 cups, 4 to 6 servings.

Gazpacho

Frosty Potage Saint-Germain

½ head lettuce, sliced
1 package (10 ounces) frozen peas
1½ cups water
¼ small onion
2 tablespoons butter or margarine
1½ teaspoons chervil
½ teaspoon salt
⅛ teaspoon pepper
1 can (10½ ounces) condensed beef broth, chilled
1 cup chilled half and half (half milk half cream)

Combine first 8 ingredients in saucepan. Cook until peas are tender, about 8 minutes. Pour into container; **GRATE (6)** 20 seconds, or until smooth. Pour into bowl. Stir in remaining ingredients. Chill. Garnish with frozen whipped cream rosettes or sour cream dollops and chopped chives. Yield: About 5¾ cups, 6 to 8 servings.

Shrimp Bisque

1 can (10 ounces) frozen cream of shrimp soup, defrosted
1½ cups milk
½ teaspoon curry powder
2 teaspoons sherry, optional

GRATE (6) all ingredients 20 seconds, or until smooth. Heat and serve hot, or chill if preferred. Garnish with small whole shrimp, if desired. Yield: About 2¾ cups, 4 servings.

CRAB BISQUE—Follow recipe for Shrimp Bisque (above). Fold **1 can (7½ ounces) crabmeat,** boned and flaked, into bisque before heating. Yield: About 3½ cups, 4 servings.

Vegetables

Corn and Bacon Pudding

See photo at right

8 slices bacon, cut in ½-inch pieces
20 soda crackers (2-inch square) broken into quarters, or ¾ cup soda cracker crumbs (page 8)
3 eggs
1½ cups milk
1 5-inch green onion, cut in 1-inch lengths
2 tablespoons bacon drippings
1 teaspoon salt
¼ teaspoon sugar
¼ teaspoon pepper
2 12-ounce cans whole kernel corn, drained
2 or 3 tomatoes, sliced and slices cut in half

Pan fry bacon until lightly browned; drain on paper toweling. Add ¼ of the cracker pieces to container at a time. Set speed at **LO (1)** then turn switch on and off quickly until crackers are coarsely chopped. Empty into bowl. Repeat 3 times. Combine eggs and milk and next 5 ingredients. **STIR (2)** until onions are coarsely chopped, about 10 seconds. Empty into mixing bowl. Quickly add the bacon, corn and crumbs. Mix. Pour into buttered shallow 2 quart casserole. Bake in moderate oven (350°F.) until set, 30 to 35 minutes. If desired garnish edge of casserole before serving with a ring of thin half tomato slices. Yield: About 6 servings.

Cabbage Wedges With Cheese Sauce

Place **6 serving-size wedges** of well drained cooked **cabbage** in heated shallow serving dish. Spoon **½ recipe of Cheese Sauce** (page 81) over wedges; save remaining sauce, if desired, to serve with cabbage. Garnish with **sliced stuffed olives,** if desired. Yield: 6 servings.

Creamed Onions and Peas in Casserole

Cook **1 package** (**10 ounces**) **frozen peas** as directed on package label. Prepare one recipe of **Quick White Sauce** (**Medium**) (page 81). Add peas and **2 jars** (**1 pound each**) **of small whole onions**, drained; heat. Pour into serving dish and sprinkle top with **buttered cereal crumbs** (page 8). Garnish with diced **pimientoes,** if desired. Yield: 6 servings.

Cauliflower With Crunchy Rarebit Sauce

Arrange a **large** well drained head of cooked **cauliflower** in warm serving dish. Spoon ½ **recipe of Blender Rarebit** (page 53) or **Cheese Sauce** (page 81) over cauliflower. Save remaining sauce to serve with vegetable. Sprinkle ¼ **cup toasted slivered almonds** over top. Yield: About 6 servings.

Creamed New Potatoes With Vegetables

Cook **1 cup** ½-inch diagonally sliced **celery** and **1 cup peas.** Prepare 1 recipe **Quick White Sauce** (**Medium**), **or Rich Cream Sauce** (**Medium**) (page 81) adding **1 5-inch green onion,** in 1-inch lengths, to sauce ingredients before cooking. **PUREE** (**4**) until finely chopped, about 5 seconds. Cook as directed in sauce recipe. Fold celery and peas into sauce and pour over **12 medium** hot, cooked **new potatoes.** Yield: 4 to 6 servings.

Vegetables Polonaise

Hot cooked **asparagus, broccoli, Brussel sprouts** and **cauliflower** are great seasoned, **buttered** and sprinkled with **buttered cereal crumbs** (page 8) and a sprinkling of chopped hard-cooked egg.

Corn and Bacon Pudding

Buttery Vegetables With a New Flavor

Try **Herb, Lemon Parsley, Onion or Watercress Butter** (page 93) on hot cooked **carrots, green or waxed beans, cauliflower or potatoes.**

Herb or Chili Butter (page 93) adds an interesting flavor on hot cooked **corn on the cob, zucchini** or **fried tomato slices.**

Italian, Garlic, Onion, Lemon Parsley or **Mustard Butter** (page 93) add great flavor to cooked **broccoli, cauliflower, cabbage** and **fried tomato slices.**

Old Fashioned Creamed Vegetables

Cooked hot **celery, broccoli, asparagus, sliced celery and peas, Brussel sprouts, carrots, cauliflower, green and wax beans, onions, mushrooms, peas and potatoes** are all delicious mixed with **Quick White Sauce (Medium)** or **Rich Cream Sauces** (page 81).

Potatoes au Gratin

Combine **1 quart** (4 cups) diced, cooked **potatoes** and **1 recipe Cheese Sauce** (page 81). Mix carefully and pour into shallow buttered 2-quart casserole. Sprinkle with ¼ **cup blender-grated Parmesan cheese** (page 100) and **paprika.** Bake in moderate oven (350°F.) for 40 minutes or until hot and bubbly. Yield: About 6 servings.

Green Beans and Bacon in Casserole

Cut **6 slices of bacon** into 1-inch pieces. Pan fry bacon until lightly browned; drain on paper toweling. Cook **2 packages** (10 ounces each) **cross cut frozen green beans** as directed on package label. Prepare **Blender Rarebit** (page 53) increasing onion to 2 slices. Combine ingredients; mix carefully. Pour into buttered 1½ quart shallow casserole. Sprinkle with **buttered corn flake crumbs** (page 8). Bake in moderate oven (350°F.) until hot and bubbly, about 20 minutes. Yield: About 6 servings.

Fifteen Great Butters

Delicious sweet and tangy butters are jiffy-made in the blender. Use them to enhance the flavor of hot toast, muffins, waffles, pancakes, sandwiches, canapés, steaks, burgers, fish and seafoods. Make the Butter Base (recipe follows) and add the ingredients desired.

Butter Base

2 tablespoons cream or milk
1 stick (½ cup) room temperature butter or margarine, sliced

STIR (2) ingredients until well mixed, 40 to 60 seconds. Stop motor and push ingredients into blades with rubber spatula as often as needed. Add ingredients needed for specific spread (see following recipes) into container, **STIR (2)** until well mixed.

HONEY BUTTER—Add ⅔ **cup honey** to Butter Base ingredients (recipe above). Spread on toast, hot biscuits, pancakes or waffles. Yield: About 1 cup.

ORANGE MARMALADE BUTTER—Add ¾ **cup thick orange marmalade** to Butter Base ingredients (recipe above). Excellent spread on toasted English muffins, hot biscuits, pancakes or used as a spread for tea sandwiches. Yield: About 1¼ cups.

BLUE CHEESE BUTTER—Add ⅓ **cup crumbled blue cheese** to Butter Base ingredients (recipe above). Spread on hot steaks or burgers. Yield: About ¾ cup.

CHILI BUTTER—Add **2 tablespoons catsup** or **chili sauce, 1 teaspoon prepared mustard, ¼ teaspoon garlic powder** and **⅛ teaspoon chili powder** to Butter Base ingredients (recipe page 92). Spread on hot steaks or burgers for a distinctively different flavor. Yield: About ½ cup.

ITALIAN BUTTER—Add **½ clove garlic,** thinly sliced, **½ teaspoon oregano** and **¼ cup shredded Parmesan cheese** to Butter Base ingredients (recipe page 92). Delicious spread on hot steaks, burgers or sliced French or Italian bread before heating. Yield: About ⅔ cup.

ONION BUTTER—Add **1 5-inch green onion,** in ½ inch slices, **1 teaspoon Worcestershire sauce** and a **dash of Tabasco sauce** to Butter Base ingredients (recipe page 92). Spread on hot steaks or burgers. Yield: About ½ cup.

WATERCRESS BUTTER—Add washed leaves (no stems) from **¼ bunch watercress** to Butter Base ingredients (recipe page 92). Use for making fancy canapés or sandwiches. Yield: About ⅔ cup.

GARLIC BUTTER—Add **½ clove garlic,** thinly sliced and **3 or 4 parsley sprigs** (no stems) to Butter Base ingredients (recipe page 92). Spread on hot steaks or burgers or on French or Italian bread slices before heating. Yield: About ½ cup.

CAPER BUTTER—Add **3 tablespoons drained bottled capers** to Butter Base ingredients (recipe page 92). Use for spreading over hot broiled or fried fish. Yield: About ⅔ cup.

CURRY CHUTNEY BUTTER — Add **½ teaspoon curry powder** and **¼ cup well-drained chutney** to Butter Base ingredients (recipe page 92). Use for spreading on hot ham or Canadian bacon. Yield: About ¾ cup.

PRALINE BUTTER—Add **⅓ cup pecan halves, ½ cup (packed) brown sugar** (broken-up) and **¼ teaspoon maple flavoring** to Butter Base ingredients (recipe page 92). Excellent spread on English muffins after toasting or before broiling. Yield: About 1¼ cups.

CINNAMON BUTTER—Add **½ cup granulated sugar** and **½ to ¾ teaspoon cinnamon** to Butter Base ingredients (recipe page 92). Fine for spreading on hot raisin, nut bread or plain toast. Yield: About 1 cup.

HERB BUTTER—Add **4 sprigs parsley** (no stems) **½ thin onion slice, ¼ teaspoon salt** and **½ teaspoon dill weed, marjoram, savory** or **oregano** to Butter Base ingredients (recipe page 92). Excellent for spreading on hot steaks or burgers or on French bread or hamburger buns before heating. Yield: About ⅔ cup.

LEMON PARSLEY BUTTER—Add **4 sprigs parsley** (no stems), **3 tablespoons lemon juice, ½ inch square of lemon peel,** sliced, and a **dash of Tabasco sauce** to Butter Base ingredients (recipe page 92). Excellent spread on hot fish or seafood. Yield: About ⅔ cup.

MUSTARD BUTTER—Add 2 **tablespoons prepared mustard** and ½ **teaspoon horseradish** to Butter Base ingredients (recipe page 92). A fine spread for bread used for making ham, corned beef, sausage or roast beef sandwiches. Yield: About ½ cup.

Baby, Junior, Senior Citizen, Health and Low Calorie Foods

BLENDER PREPARED FOODS LET BABIES, TODDLERS, SENIOR CITIZENS, CONVALESCENTS AND WEIGHT WATCHERS EAT BETTER THAN EVER AND SAVES MONEY AS WELL

Baby Vegetables and Meats

⅓ cup milk
1 cup drained well cooked or canned vegetables or finely diced cooked meats
Dash of salt

CHOP (**8**) ingredients in container until perfectly smooth, about 30 seconds. Stop motor, as needed, and push ingredients into blades with rubber spatula. Test for smoothness by rubbing a small amount between fingers. Yield: About 1 cup, 2 servings.

Baby Fruits

¼ cup fruit juice or fruit syrup
1 cup cooked dried or fresh or canned fruit
Sugar, as desired

Prepare same as vegetables (above). Yield: About 1 cup, 2 servings.

Ham Patties (page 96)

Junior or Toddler Foods

Follow recipes for Baby Foods (page 94) and **WHIP (5)** 15 to 20 seconds or to coarseness desired.

Convalescent and Fluid Diet Foods

Lump-free tasty fruits, vegetables and meats can be prepared easily. Follow recipes for baby foods (page 94) or any of the following:

Quick Cook Custard

Follow recipe for Custard (page 44). Instead of baking custards in oven cover each dish with aluminum foil and arrange on rack in a skillet filled to rack level with hot water. Cover skillet and cook custards until metal knife inserted in center comes out clean, 25 to 30 minutes. Chill.

Eggnog

2 eggs
2 tablespoons sugar
1 cup chilled milk
¾ teaspoon vanilla
⅛ teaspoon salt
1 cup chilled half and half (half milk half cream) or milk
½ cup whipped cream or dessert topping, optional
Nutmeg

STIR (2) first 5 ingredients until well mixed, 4 to 6 seconds. Stir in half and half or milk. Pour into punch cups or glasses. If desired, garnish top with whipped cream or dessert topping or nutmeg. Yield: About 2¼ cups; 2 to 4 servings.

Holiday Eggnog

Follow recipe for Eggnog (above) and stir ½ to **⅔ cup brandy** into mixture before garnishing. Yield: About 5 cups; 10 servings.

Quick Breakfast Shake

1½ cups cold water
1 cup crushed ice
½ of 6 ounce can frozen orange, tangerine, boysenberry, or grape juice, partially defrosted
2 eggs
⅔ cup non-fat dry milk solids
*¼ cup sugar**

Combine ingredients in container. **STIR (2)** until well mixed, 3 to 5 seconds. Serve at once. Yield: About 3¼ cups, 2 or 3 large drinks.

*Substitute liquid artificial sweetener, to taste, for sugar, if desired.

Fruited-Oat Breakfast Drink

2 cups well chilled milk
¾ cup cooled cooked, quick cooking, rolled oats (can be left-over cooked oats)
2 tablespoons sugar
1 teaspoon vanilla
1 package (10 ounces) frozen strawberries, raspberries, boysenberries, or peaches, partially defrosted and cubed

Combine first 4 ingredients in container. **STIR (2)** until well mixed, 3 to 4 seconds. Add fruit; **STIR (2)** until well mixed, 4 to 6 seconds. Yield: About 1 quart, 3 to 4 servings.

Whole-Grain Wheat Bread

Follow Yeast Bread recipe (page 31); change as follows. **BLEND (10) 1½ cups whole wheat grains** in container until very fine, 40 to 60 seconds; pour into bowl. Proceed as for Yeast Bread. Decrease flour to (about) 4 cups. Substitute **brown** for granulated **sugar,** increase shortening to ⅓ cup, and add **2 eggs,** one at a time, to milk mixture in container through top opening, while motor is running.

WHEAT GERM BREAD—Follow recipe for **Yeast Bread;** (page 31) substitute **1 cup wheat germ** for 1 cup flour.

WHOLE WHEAT BREAD—Follow Yeast Bread recipe; (page 31) substitute **brown** for granulated **sugar** and **3 cups whole wheat** flour for 3 cups of wheat flour.

Banana Wheat Germ Muffins

1½ cups sifted flour
⅓ cup sugar
3 teaspoons baking powder
¾ teaspoon salt
½ cup wheat germ
⅔ cup milk
2 eggs
¼ cup soft butter or margarine
1 medium banana, in 1-inch slices

Combine and sift first 4 ingredients in mixing bowl. Stir in wheat germ. Combine remaining ingredients in container. Set speed at **GRATE** (**6**) then switch motor on and off quickly until banana slices are well chopped, about 8 to 10 times. Pour into dry ingredients. Mix just until dry ingredients are moistened. Fill well-greased and floured or paper lined muffin pans ⅔ full. Bake in hot oven (400°F.) until done and lightly browned, 20 to 25 minutes. Yield: About 12 medium muffins.

Date Wheat Germ Muffins

Follow recipe for Banana Wheat Germ Muffins (above) and change as follows. Use ⅓ instead of ½ cup wheat germ. Increase milk to 1 cup, butter or margarine to ⅓ cup, omit bananas and add **2 1-inch squares of lemon rind,** quartered and **½ cup pitted dates,** cut in half and processed with milk and eggs. Mix and bake as directed for Banana Wheat Germ Muffins. Yield: 12 muffins.

Ham Patties

See photo page 94

½ pound ground fully-cooked ham
½ cup blender-made bread crumbs (page 100)
¼ cup salad dressing
1 teaspoon prepared mustard
3 tablespoons honey
1 tablespoon pineapple syrup
1 pineapple ring

Combine first 4 ingredients; mix. Shape into two patties, 1-inch thick. Mix honey and syrup. Broil patties 4 inches from heat source about 7 minutes per side. Brush with honey mixture during broiling. Garnish each with ½ pineapple slice. Yield: 2 servings.

Spinach Soufflé with Blender Rarebit

*2 packages (10 ounces each) frozen leaf spinach**
1¾ cups milk
3 eggs
½ thin slice onion
3 tablespoons melted butter or margarine
2 tablespoons lemon juice
3 tablespoons flour
1 teaspoon salt
Dash pepper
Blender Rarebit (page 53)

Cook spinach as directed on package label. Drain well. Combine all ingredients, except Blender Rarebit, in container. **CHOP** (**8**) until spinach is coarsely chopped, about 10 seconds. Pour into well-buttered 1½ quart casserole. Bake in pan of hot shallow water in a moderate oven (375°F.) 50 to 55 minutes or until metal knife inserted in center comes out clean. Let stand 5 minutes; cut into 6 portions and serve with Blender Rarebit. Yield: 6 servings.

*Substitute 1½ cups well drained cooked fresh spinach, if desired.

Carrot Soufflé

Follow recipe for Spinach Soufflé (above) and make the following few changes. Substitute **2 cups** cooked sliced (¼-inch) drained **carrots** for spinach; increase onion to 1 slice and omit Blender Rarebit. Delicious with Quick White Sauce (Medium) (page 81). Yield: 6 servings.

Apricot or Prune Whip

1 cup dried apricots or pitted prunes
⅔ cup hot water
⅓ cup sugar
2 thin slices unpeeled lemon
1½ cups whipped cream or dessert topping

Combine first 4 ingredients in saucepan. Bring to a boil; cover and simmer gently 20 minutes. Cool. Pour into container; **CHOP** (**8**) until mixture is smooth. Pour into bowl; fold in 1¼ cups whipped cream or dessert topping. Pile into sherbet glasses. Top with remaining whipped cream or dessert topping. Yield: 4 servings.

Chilled Tomato Bouillon Squares

¼ cup cold tomato juice
1 envelope (1 tablespoon) unflavored gelatin
¾ cup hot (simmering) tomato juice
1 beef or chicken bouillon cube
¼-inch slice unpeeled lemon, quartered
1 thin slice onion
Dash of pepper
2 or 3 drops liquid artificial sweetener, or to taste
3 ice cubes or ½ cup ice water

Add cold tomato juice to container. Add gelatin. Set speed at **STIR** (**2**) then switch motor on and off. Let stand 5 minutes. Add hot tomato juice and bouillon cube. **STIR** (**2**) until gelatin is dissolved, 3 to 5 seconds. Add next 4 ingredients; **STIR** (**2**) until lemon rind is finely chopped about 8 seconds. Add ice cubes; **STIR** (**2**) until melted, 2 to 3 seconds. Pour into oiled 8 x 8 x 2 inch pan. Chill until firm. Cut into 1-inch squares; pile into chilled bouillon cup. Top with Low Calorie Mock Sour Cream (below); garnish with chopped fresh cucumber and chopped chives, if desired. Yield: 3 to 4 servings.

Low Calorie Mock Sour Cream

Combine **⅓ cup skimmed or whole milk, 1 cup** (**8 ounce**) **creamed cottage cheese, 1 tablespoon vinegar or lemon juice** and **⅛ teaspoon salt** in container. **BLEND** (**10**) just until smooth, about 25 seconds. Stop motor; push ingredients into blades with rubber spatula, as necessary. Use on vegetables, for making dips, on salads, or meats. Yield; 1 cup.

Sour Cream or Yogurt Dressing

1 cup yogurt or dairy sour cream
3 tablespoons vinegar
1 thin slice onion, cut in half
¼ teaspoon salt
2 teaspoons honey
¼ pimiento

CHOP (**8**) ingredients in container until onion is finely chopped, 5 to 6 seconds. Yield: About 1¼ cups.

Low Calorie Salad Dressing or Basting Sauce

1 cup tomato juice or sauce
2 tablespoons lemon juice
1 thin slice onion
1 teaspoon prepared mustard
¼ teaspoon salt
½ teaspoon celery salt
2 dashes Tabasco Sauce
2 teaspoons Worcestershire sauce
4 to 6 drops liquid artificial sweetener, or to taste

Combine ingredients in container; **STIR** (**2**) until onion is finely chopped, 4 to 5 seconds. Use as salad dressing or basting sauce for meat. Yield: About 1 cup.

Pineapple Carrot Salad

1 cup unsweetened orange or pineapple juice
1½ envelopes (1½ tablespoons) unflavored gelatin
¾ cup boiling water
2 tablespoons vinegar or lemon juice
¼ teaspoon salt
½ cup ¼-inch thick carrot slices
½ cup well drained crushed pineapple
½ cup well drained small orange chunks
½ teaspoon liquid artificial sweetener, or to taste

Pour ⅓ cup orange or pineapple juice into container. Add gelatin. Set speed at **STIR** (**2**) then switch motor on and off. Let stand 5 minutes. Add boiling water. **STIR** (**2**) until gelatin is dissolved, 3 to 5 seconds. Add vinegar or lemon juice, remaining ¾ cup chilled orange or pineapple juice, salt and carrot slices to container. **STIR** (**2**) until carrots are finely chopped, 10 to 15 seconds. Pour into bowl and add pineapple and orange. Stir in artificial sweetener, chill until syrupy. Pour into oiled 8 x 8 x 2 inch pan, chill until firm. Cut into squares; serve on crisp lettuce and top with Low Calorie Mock Sour Cream (at left), if desired. Yield: About 4 servings.

Islands Milk Shake

2 cups chilled buttermilk
1 can (8¾ ounces) crushed pineapple, undrained
1 medium banana, in 1-inch slices
6 to 8 maraschino cherries
⅓ cup sugar or 8 to 10 drops liquid sweetener
Mint sprigs, optional

WHIP (**5**) ingredients 10 seconds. Pour into 4 tall glasses. Garnish with mint, if desired. Yield: About 3¼ cups, 3 to 4 servings.

Fruity Fizz

1 package (10 ounces) frozen peaches, strawberries, raspberries or blueberries, partially defrosted and cubed
2 tablespoons non-fat dry milk solids
½ cup water
1 pint dietetic vanilla ice cream, cubed
2 bottles (10 ounces each) chilled low calorie gingerale
Mint sprigs, optional

GRATE (**6**) first 4 ingredients 15 seconds. Pour an equal amount of mixture into 4 or 6 tall glasses. Fill with gingerale; stir gently. Garnish with mint, if desired. Yield: About 5½ cups; 4 to 5 servings.

Low-Cal Fruit Shake

1 can (1 pound) diet apricot halves, undrained
½ cup water
¼ cup non-fat dry milk solids
½ pint dietetic vanilla ice cream, cubed

PUREE (**4**) ingredients 20 seconds, or until well mixed. Pour into tall glasses. Yield: About 3⅔ cups, 4 to 5 servings.

Low-Cal Cocoa

Follow **Hot Cocoa recipe** (page 21); use hot **skimmed** instead of whole **milk.** Omit sugar and stir in favorite **artificial sweetener** to taste after blending. Garnish, if desired, with **artificially sweetened whipped dessert topping.** Yield: About 2¼ cups, 2 to 3 servings.

Special Tricks

Time Saving Blender

The lucky homemaker with a blender finds food preparation jobs are easily completed in **seconds** rather than **minutes**! Keep the blender handy for quick use every meal of the day as well as afternoon and evening snacks.

Speedy Cheese Sauces

Cut **American, Cheddar or Swiss cheese** into ½ inch cubes or pieces. Pour very hot Quick White or Rich Cream Sauce (page 81) from saucepan into container. Cover. Set speed at **STIR** (**2**); turn motor on and add cheese pieces as desired through top opening, rapidly, 1 at a time, to sauce. Reheat sauce, if needed.

To Make Small Amounts Of Confectioners' Sugar

Pour ½ cup granulated sugar into container; cover. Process at **HI** (**13**) 60 to 70 seconds. Let stand with cover on for 30 seconds until sugar settles. Rest motor 2 minutes before repeating. Yield: About ⅔ cup.

Satin Smooth Sauces Galore

Sauces are satin smooth when prepared in blender. See pages 81 through 85 for recipes. To eliminate lumpy sauces pour hot mixture into container and **PUREE** (**4**) until smooth. Reheat, if desired.

Gravy Lumpy? Blend It!

Pour lumpy gravy into container; **STIR** (**2**) until smooth. Reheat, if necessary.

Pancake and Popover Mixes

Follow directions on label of favorite pancake or popover mix. Pour liquids and eggs, if used, into container first. **STIR** (**2**) just until well mixed. Do not overblend. Bake as directed on package.

Speedy Crushed Ice For Many Uses

Very finely crushed ice is made quickly and easily. Fill container ½ to ⅔ full with ice cubes. Add water needed to fill container to 4 cup level. **GRATE** (**6**) until ice is very finely chopped. Drain; use at once for making iced drinks, soups, desserts, chilling foods in a hurry, keeping relishes, butter or other foods cool, or for scores of therapeutic uses. For better results use ice crusher attachment.

Unflavored Gelatin

For each (1 tablespoon) envelope of gelatin used, pour ½ cup cold water into container. Add gelatin. Let stand 5 minutes to soften. Heat 1½ cups liquid to boiling stage. Add to gelatin. Set speed at **LO** (**1**) then switch motor on and off until gelatin is dissolved, about 6 or 7 times.

Flavored Gelatin

Empty contents of package of flavored gelatin into container. Heat the amount of liquid required to boiling point. Pour into container and process at **LO** (**1**) until gelatin is dissolved, 5 to 8 seconds.

Be A Soap Saver!

Save ends of bars of hand or facial soap to make into fine liquid soap for washing delicate garments, shampooing, etc. Cube odds and ends of soap. Drop into container. Add 1½ cups boiling water for each cup of cubed soap used. Let stand 3 to 5 minutes. Set speed at **STIR** (**2**) then switch motor on and off just until soap is dissolved. Cool, store in jars. Same procedure may be followed with ends of laundry soap bars.

Quick Chilled Drinks

Fill container ⅓ full of ice cubes or crushed ice. Fill with liquid (water, strong tea or coffee brew, artificially flavored non-carbonated fruit drink). **CHOP** (**8**) just until liquid is chilled.

Instant Puddings

Pour milk or liquid, recommended on label of package of favorite instant pudding, into container. Add pudding **STIR** (**2**) until mixed, about 10 seconds. Pour into serving dishes. Chill 5 to 10 minutes before serving.

Creamy Frosting Mixes

Use ingredients called for in package directions for creamy frostings, not egg white or fluffy frostings. Put soft butter or margarine and water into container. Set speed at **STIR** (**2**). Cover. Start motor; add frosting mix gradually through top opening. Stop motor; push ingredients into blades with rubber spatula, as needed. Turn speed to **BLEND** (**10**) when mixture begins to thicken. Stop motor; push ingredients into blades with rubber spatula, as needed. Yield: Fills and frosts two 8-inch layers or one 13 x 9 x 1½ inch cake.

Instant Potatoes

Use ingredients suggested on package label for the quantity desired. Add measured boiling water and salt to container. Set speed at **PUREE** (**4**), cover. Turn motor on and add dehydrated potato in fine stream through top opening, about 25 seconds. Add butter and milk and **PUREE** (**4**) until desired consistency, about 20 seconds.

Reconstitute Dry Milk Solids

Use proportions of non-fat dry milk solids and cold water suggested on label of favorite non-fat dry milk solids. Let stand 2 to 3 minutes before processing. **PUREE** (**4**) just until well mixed, 2 to 5 seconds. Let stand a few minutes before serving.

Jiffy Sauces for Desserts

Chocolate and butterscotch chips melt jiffy-quick in hot liquid in the blender. See page 85 for Fudge Sauce and Butterscotch Dessert Sauce.

Grated Hard Cheeses

Cut Parmesan cheese (or other hard cheeses) into ½-inch cubes. **GRATE** (**6**) ½ cup of cubes at a time. Add cubes to container **GRATE** (**6**) to desired degree of fineness, about 15 seconds for moderately fine grated cheese. Yield: About 5 ounces of Parmesan cheese is required to make 1 cup grated Parmesan cheese.

Chopped Natural Cheeses

Cut natural Cheddar, American or Swiss cheese into ½-inch cubes. Chill cubes very well (in freezer, if desired) a few minutes. Add ½ cup cheese cubes to container at a time. Set speed at **STIR** (**2**), then switch motor on and off quickly 5 times or until desired degree of fineness.

Chopped Nuts

Chop a few shelled nuts at a time. Pour ½ cup pecan or walnut halves, shelled peanuts, whole hazelnuts or halved Brazil nuts into container. Set speed at **STIR** (**2**); switch motor on and off quickly until chopped to desired fineness. Empty container; repeat as needed.

Chopped Candy

Many a dessert, sundae sauce and confection is made with chopped candy. See page 9 for chopping directions.

Lumpy Brown Sugar?

Break brown sugar lumps into ½ to ¾-inch pieces, using rolling pin, if needed. Place sugar lumps, ½ cup at a time, in blender container and set at **STIR** (**2**) and process until lumps are gone.

Prepare Cake Mixes Easily

See directions on page 32.

Frozen Fruit-Ades (Lemonade, Punch, Etc.)

Prepare as for Fast Fix Juice concentrates, see page 21.

Chopping Vegetables

Chopping cooked and raw vegetables has always been a slow and tedious task. Not so if they are blender-chopped.

Vegetables can be chopped fine enough to serve the baby or invalid requiring smooth or fine textured vegetables.

Vegetable soufflés are no trick either for the vegetables can be chopped fine enough to keep them light, airy and high.

Crisp vegetables for Old Fashioned Coleslaw chop quickly and beautifully the water-chop way. See page 77 for complete directions.

Bread Crumbs

DRY OR SOFT BREAD CRUMBS—Tear or break bread slice into sixths; add to container. Set speed at **HI** (**13**) then quickly switch motor on and off 2 times, more if finer crumbs are desired. Yield: 1 slice of bread makes about ½ cup crumbs.

BUTTERED BREAD CRUMBS—Buttered bread crumbs can easily be made by spreading soft butter on the bread before tearing it into pieces. Process as directed above.

Crumbs for Countless Uses

Cracker, cookie and cereal crumbs are in demand in kitchens of good cooks. It takes little time, effort and cleaning-up when crumbs are blender-made. See page 8 for directions.

Fast Fix Juices (From Frozen Concentrates)

See page 21 for directions.

Frozen Concentrated Soups

Hold can of frozen soup under water until contents are partially defrosted. Open can; empty soup into container. Add liquid recommended on label. Run at **LO** (**1**) until mixed, 15 to 20 seconds. Pour into saucepan and heat.

Fritters

Dessert Fritter Batter

1½ cups sifted flour
¼ cup sugar
2 teaspoons baking powder
¾ teaspoon salt
2 eggs
¾ cup milk
1 tablespoon cooking oil

Sift first 4 ingredients into bowl. **STIR** (**2**) eggs, milk and oil in container until well mixed, about 5 seconds. Add dry ingredients; mix at **LO** (**1**) 5 to 8 seconds, or until smooth. Stop motor; push ingredients into blades, as needed. Use for making apple, peach, orange (below) or other fruit fritters. Yield: About 1½ cups batter.

APPLE FRITTERS (at right)—Peel, core and cut **4 apples** into rings ½-inch thick. Dust slices lightly with flour. Dip, a few slices at a time, into **Dessert Fritter Batter** (above) and fry in **hot oil** (375°F.) **about 2 inches deep,** until fritters are a golden brown on both sides, 3 to 4 minutes. Turn once during frying. Drain on paper toweling. Sprinkle with **confectioners' or cinnamon sugar,** as desired. Serve hot. Yield: About 4 servings.

ORANGE FRITTERS—Use **Dessert Fritter Batter** (above) and prepare same as Apple Fritters (above) substituting **4 medium to large peeled navel oranges** for apples. Cut oranges in ½-inch slices. Sprinkle with **confectioners' sugar** or serve with **Orange Sauce** (page 84). Yield: About 4 servings.

PEACH FRITTERS—Use **Dessert Fritter Batter** (above) and prepare same as Apple Fritters (above) substituting **8 large well-drained canned peach halves,** cut in half, for apple. Proceed as for Apple Fritters. Sprinkle with **confectioners' sugar,** or drizzle with **Butterscotch Dessert, Butterscotch Pecan** or **Fudge Sauce** (page 85). Yield: About 4 servings.

BASIC FRITTER BATTER—Follow recipe for **Dessert Fritter Batter,** (at left) and reduce sugar to 1 tablespoon. Use for coating seafoods, vegetables, etc. Yield: About 1½ cups batter.

French Fried Shrimp

Stir ½ **teaspoon curry powder** into **Basic Fritter Batter** (above). Coat large **cooked cleaned shrimp** with batter. Fry, a few at a time, in hot oil (375°F.) about 2 inches deep. Fry a golden brown, 3 to 4 minutes; turn once. Drain well. Serve with **Seafood Cocktail Sauce** (page 84). Yield: Batter for 2 pounds large shrimp.

CORN FRITTERS—Stir **1 can** (**12 ounces**) **kernel corn,** drained, into **Basic Fritter Batter** (above). Drop tablespoonfuls of batter, one at a time, into deep hot oil (375°F.) Brown on both sides, about 4 minutes. Turn once. Drain. Serve hot, plain or with syrup. Yield: About 4 servings.

Apple Fritters

Index

A

B

C

Q

R

S

T

V

W

Remove chart by tearing along perforations.

Blender Speed Conversion Chart

RECIPE SPEEDS IN "BLENDER COOKING" BOOK

The recipes in **"Blender Cooking"** use a speed range from 1 to 13. Speeds are shown in **LARGER** type. **If your blender** does not have 13 speeds you will need a cross-reference. The chart below (after you complete the outer portion for **your** blender speeds) will be your cross-reference.

COMPLETING THE RECIPE SPEED CHART FOR YOUR BLENDER

1. If your blender speed settings **are on** the chart below:
   Find the section of the chart that has the same number of speeds as your blender. Extend the lines between the various speeds out to the outer blank section of the chart. Write in **your** blender settings in the spaces in the outer section. Chart is now ready to use.
2. If your blender's speeds **are not on** the chart below:
   Divide the outer blank section into the same number of spaces as speeds on your blender. Write in your blender settings in the spaces in the outer section. Chart is now ready to use.

HOW TO USE THE COMPLETED CHART

1. Find the **recipe speed** in the portion of the chart titled **"Recipe Speeds In This Book."**
2. Use **your** speed in the outer area opposite **"Recipe Speeds In This Book."** (You may even want to write **your** speed on the recipe itself.)
3. Fill out this chart and place it near your blender work area for future reference.

Ring	Settings
MY OWN BLENDER SETTINGS	
13 RECIPE SPEEDS IN THIS BOOK	LO (1), STIR (2), CRUMB (3), PUREE (4), WHIP (5), GRATE (6), MIX (7), CHOP (8), GRIND (9), BLEND (10), LIQUEFY (11), FRAPPÉ (12), HI (13)
16 SPEED BLENDER SETTING	LO (1), (2), (3), (4), (5), (6), (7), (8), (9), (10), (11), (12), (13), (14), (15), HI (16)
14 SPEED BLENDER SETTING	LO (1), (2), (3), (4), (5), (6), (7), (8), (9), (10), (11), (12), (13), HI (14)
10 SPEED BLENDER SETTING	STIR, PUREE, WHIP, GRATE, MIX, CHOP, GRIND, BLEND, LIQUEFY, FRAPPÉ
8 SPEED BLENDER SETTING	STIR, PUREE, WHIP, GRATE, MIX, CHOP, BLEND, LIQUEFY
7 SPEED BLENDER SETTING	STIR, WHIP, GRATE, MIX, CHOP, BLEND, LIQUEFY
5 SPEED BLENDER SETTING	LO (1), (2), (3), (4), HI (5)
3 SPEED BLENDER SETTING	LO, MED, HI
2 SPEED BLENDER SETTING	LO, HI

Handy chart permits you to convert your blender speeds to approximate those used in this book.